Privilege Lost

Privilege Lost

*Who Leaves the Upper Middle Class
and How They Fall*

JESSI STREIB

OXFORD

UNIVERSITY PRESS

OXFORD
UNIVERSITY PRESS

Oxford University Press is a department of the University of Oxford. It furthers
the University's objective of excellence in research, scholarship, and education
by publishing worldwide. Oxford is a registered trade mark of Oxford University
Press in the UK and certain other countries.

Published in the United States of America by Oxford University Press
198 Madison Avenue, New York, NY 10016, United States of America.

© Oxford University Press 2020

Library of Congress Cataloging-in-Publication Data
Names: Streib, Jessi, author.
Title: Privilege lost : who leaves the upper middle class and how they fall / by Jessi Streib.
Description: New York, NY : Oxford University Press, [2020] | Includes bibliographical
references and index.
Identifiers: LCCN 2019042460 (print) | LCCN 2019042461 (ebook) |
ISBN 9780190854041 (hardback) | ISBN 9780190854058 (paperback) |
ISBN 9780190854072 (epub) | ISBN 9780190854089
Subjects: LCSH: Marginality, Social—United States—History. | Downward mobility (Social sciences)—
United States—History. | Youth—United States—History. | Middle class—United States—History. |
Whites—Race identity—United States—History.
Classification: LCC HM1136 .S78 2020 (print) | LCC HM1136 (ebook) |
DDC 305.5/130973—dc23
LC record available at https://lccn.loc.gov/2019042460
LC ebook record available at https://lccn.loc.gov/2019042461

1 3 5 7 9 8 6 4 2

Paperback printed by Marquis, Canada
Hardback printed by Bridgeport National Bindery, Inc., United States of America

Contents

Privilege Lost

1

The Downwardly Mobile

Julie,[1] a petite, slender young woman with long curly blonde hair, was among the approximately 20% of white Americans who were born into the upper-middle class in the mid- to late 1980s[2]—a group composed of youth with at least one college-educated professional parent.[3] Born near the top of the class structure, she was also born at a particularly advantageous moment:[4] a time when college-educated professional parents' incomes rose,[5] wealth soared,[6] and when they invested far more time and money in their children.[7] Academics, journalists, and ordinary people alike feared what these changes would produce: a social class system that locked upper-middle-class children into their class of birth while locking everyone else out.[8] Had they followed Julie's trajectory from teenager to young adult, it would have not have allayed their fears. Julie sailed through high school and college then on to a job as a media planner at an advertising agency. By age 28, Julie had been promoted four times and worked as an associate media director—a position that kept her in the upper-middle class. Her long-term boyfriend would likely seal her place there. Like most college-educated professionals, she planned to marry someone like her—another professional with a college degree.[9]

Julie's story is one that social scientists and journalists commonly tell—one of upper-middle-class youth becoming upper-middle-class adults.[10] But the focus on Julie's story overshadows stories like Vera's—ones that are just as common but rarely told. Vera was a bubbly woman with brown hair and freckles who was also born into the upper-middle class during the 1980s—the time when college-educated professional parents increased their efforts to keep their children in their class.[11] Yet, Vera's trajectory diverged from Julie's. After finishing high school, Vera attended a community college and planned to later transfer to a four-year college. She acquired an associate's degree, but, at age 28, she had not obtained a bachelor's degree and no longer thought she would. She became an office assistant and married a high-school-educated electrical lineman. Her story was one of downward mobility—she entered adulthood in a lower social class than the one she was born into as a child.

Privilege Lost. Jessi Streib, Oxford University Press (2020) © Oxford University Press.
DOI: 10.1093/oso/9780190854041.001.0001

This book follows over 100 youth like Julie and Vera—youth born into the upper-middle class—as they transition from teens to young adults in ways that shape their class trajectory. As youth move through the institutions that mark their teenage and young adult years—school, college, work, and marriage—they move from a period when their class position is defined by their parents' education and occupation to a time when their class position is also defined by their own. Some youth, like Julie, emerge from this life stage poised to remain in the upper-middle class. Others, like Vera, emerge already falling from it. This book documents the difference. Among white upper-middle-class youth—those for whom racial discrimination cannot easily explain their fall—it reveals who is downwardly mobile, how they fall, and why they rarely see it coming.[12]

What Is Downward Mobility?

If the class structure resembles a pyramid, those in the upper-middle class are part of a narrow band near the top. A four-year college degree and professional job define membership in this social class, and only about one in five white American children have at least one parent with these statuses. Being born near the top of the class structure has many advantages, but it also has another important feature: there is plenty of room to fall.

"Downward mobility" refers to falling—moving from a higher to a lower social class. It is a neutral descriptor—not a moral or negative one. There are many types of downward mobility. This book focuses on one: intergenerational, absolute downward mobility from the upper-middle class. Intergenerational downward mobility refers to adult children entering a lower social class than their parents occupied as adults. As children's class position is defined by their parents' class position, intergenerational downward mobility also refers to entering a lower social class as an adult than the class individuals were raised in as a child. Intergenerational mobility is measured in what social scientists call an "absolute" way when it refers to children entering a lower social class than their parents, regardless of how they or their parents rank compared with their peers in their generation.[13] As every upper-middle-class youth has at least one college-educated parent and may also have one parent who entered the upper-middle class through marriage, downward mobility from the upper-middle class means neither becoming a college-educated professional *nor* marrying one. Class reproduction for youth born into the upper-middle class, by contrast, means becoming a college-educated professional *or* marrying one.[14]

Of course, class positions can change, and some argue that they are especially prone to do so shortly after the transition to adulthood.[15] This book follows youth from age 13 to 18 until age 23 to 28 and takes this concern into account in three ways. First, because some young adults are still completing their education, this book defines graduate school as equivalent to a professional job. Second, because young adults' incomes are particularly unstable, only education and occupation are used to define class.[16] And, third, this book considers youths' *trajectories* toward downward mobility or class reproduction, not their final or permanent class positions. These trajectories are relevant to youth's future. About 80% of upper-middle-class youth who avoid downward mobility at age 26 continue to avoid it as middle-aged adults,[17] and about 70% of upper-middle-class youth on downwardly mobile trajectories at age 26 continue to be downwardly mobile around age 40.[18] Thus, contrary to folklore, the transition to adulthood is not a time of inconsequential exploration—even for those born into the upper-middle class. Rather, it sets youth on trajectories that most do not leave.

The Numbers

For youth born in the 1980s, the most common way to enter the upper-middle class as an adult was to be born into it as a child. However, among this cohort, downwardly mobile trajectories were common too.[19] About half of children born to a college-educated parent in the 1980s have not graduated from college,[20] and over half of the sons of professionals have not become professionals.[21] Even when including marriage as a way to stay in one's class, about half of youth born in the upper-middle class have not reproduced their childhood class position.[22]

Downward mobility is then routine. Part of the reason relates to the number of slots in the upper-middle class—the number of students colleges admit, the number of professional jobs, and the number of college-educated professionals available to marry.[23] For upper-middle-class youth born in the 1980s, only the first part of this pathway had plenty of positions. American colleges have long reserved space for upper-middle-class students and they continued to do so as Julie and Vera's cohort applied.[24] Selective colleges admitted students using criteria that tilted in upper-middle-class students' favor: the courses offered in highly resourced schools, the test scores that pricy school districts made easier for upper-middle-class students to obtain, the extracurricular activities upper-middle-class families could afford, the tuition checks their parents promised to write, and their parents' receipt of certain college degrees.[25] In addition, for Julie and Vera's cohort, positions in colleges became easier to obtain as most four-year colleges became less selective, with elite universities being the only exceptions.[26] The increasing availability of student loans also allowed more upper-middle-class youth to attend college, even if they would need to pay them off later.[27]

However, the labor market did not maintain so many professional positions for youth born in the 1980s. This cohort was new to the labor force when the Great Recession hit—a time when employers took down job ads, layoffs rose, and competition for jobs increased.[28] And, while the Great Recession struck in dramatic fashion, other troubling economic trends had long been underway. As more people received college and graduate degrees, the number of professional jobs did not also expand. Instead, more highly educated people were pushed into nonprofessional jobs.[29] The image of the college-educated barista arose to reflect this new reality—even after the Great Recession officially ended, many recent college graduates spent their 20s without professional work.[30]

Moreover, for youth born in the 1980s, it was becoming more difficult to secure a spot in the upper-middle class through marriage. Compared with the past generation, a larger portion of upper-middle-class workers chose other upper-middle-class workers as their spouse; marrying laterally by social class became more common and marrying up by social class became harder to do.[31] In addition, college-educated professionals increasingly turned their backs on early marriage. Even if some youth could marry up, they were unlikely to do so as young adults.[32]

The number of professional jobs and marriage partners helps explain why staying in the upper-middle class is difficult to do—even for youth born into it. However, knowing this tells us little about *who* is apt to fall, *how* they fall, and *why* they don't see it coming.[33] The latter questions are the focus of this book. To answer them we need to study downward mobility in a new way.

Who Falls and How

This book develops a new framework to understand who falls and how.[34] It does so by analyzing interviews with 107 white youth born into the

upper-middle class between 1984 and 1990.[35] Detailed information about
the data is available in the methodological and tables appendices, but for now
it is important to know a few simple facts. Each respondent participated in a
nationally representative survey. From this group, researchers used a quota
sample to select respondents to complete up to four in-depth interviews.
These interviews occurred every two to three years over a 10 year period—
all when respondents transitioned from teenagers to young adults. The
interviewed respondents do not perfectly represent white upper-middle-
class American youth but do depict aspects of their diversity—they come
from 35 states, from big cities and small towns, and from many types of
schools. Of the interviewed youth, 53% are on class reproduction trajectories
while 47% are on downwardly mobile trajectories—a rate similar to the mobility trajectories of white upper-middle-class American youth of the same
cohort and age.[36]

Below is an overview of how we can think about who falls and how; the
following chapters provide concrete tales that adhere to this account. The
overview first describes the framework's two main concepts—inherited resources and identities—as well as each of their subparts. It then explains how
inherited resources and identities relate to downward mobility. Of course,
this new framework does not capture all reasons for downward mobility,
describe all upper-middle class youth's lives, or allow us to be certain that a
particular person will be downwardly mobile. It does, however, describe the
lives of the majority of youth in the sample—and likely a majority of white
upper-middle-class Americans' class trajectories too.[37]

Inherited Resources

To understand who falls, we need to understand youths' inherited resources.
Each upper-middle-class youth is raised with a set of *inherited resources*—
a constellation of economic capital (money), human capital (academic
knowledge and skills), and cultural capital (knowledge of how to navigate
institutions)[38] that parents pass down to their children and that their children
accept.[39] Each of these resources matter for social mobility because of how
schools, colleges, professional workplaces, and professional spouses evaluate
people with them.[40] Money matters for mobility because it buys access to
better schools and because schools, colleges, and professional workplaces
reward the opportunities that money buys.[41] Academic and institutional

knowledge matter because schools, colleges, and workplaces not only teach them but also reward those who learn them at home. Students who enter school with academic knowledge their parents taught them are deemed smarter, those with knowledge of how to navigate school are deemed better students, and both are given opportunities to learn more than youth whose parents taught them less.[42] And, as most college-educated professionals now look to marry other college-educated professionals, upper-middle-class suitors tend to choose spouses based upon their money, academic skills, and institutional knowledge too.[43] These resources then matter because they help youth become college-educated professionals and marry them—they help youth remain in the upper-middle class.

Of course, not all upper-middle-class parents possess equal amounts of each resource. Parents' earnings vary, even within the upper-middle class.[44] Parents' human and cultural capital varies too. Some upper-middle-class parents are college-educated professionals who have considerable experience gaining academic skills and navigating institutions. Some upper-middle-class parents are not college-educated professionals but obtained their class position through marriage—in Julie's and Vera's parents' generation it was more common for college-educated professionals to marry spouses without college degrees and professional jobs.[45] Nonprofessionals' occupations give them less human and cultural capital, and, for those without four-year college degrees, their educations confer less human and cultural capital too.

Parents also vary in how actively they transfer resources to their children. While economic capital can be simply passed down,[46] human and cultural capital must be actively transferred through hands-on parenting.[47] Some youth have college-educated professional parents who are hands-on—parents who are equipped to pass down information about school, college, and professional work and whom their children say actively transfer their knowledge about these topics. Other youth have college-educated professional parents who are hands-off. Youth say that these parents do not talk to them about school, college, or professional work—doing less to actively transfer their academic and institutional knowledge. Parents can be hands-off for a variety of reasons—due to, for instance, a preferred parenting style, work commitments, health issues, or divorce.[48] And, of course, not all youth are positioned to accept the resources their parents pass down. Some youth have learning difficulties, physical illnesses, and mental health conditions that make it difficult for them to internalize or use the resources their parents provide.[49]

The first step to understanding who falls is then to recognize that upper-middle-class youth grow up with varied resources. Some upper-middle-class youth inherit *resource weaknesses*—they receive or are able to accept little human, cultural, or economic capital from their parents compared with their peers in their social class. Other upper-middle-class youth inherit *resource strengths*—compared with their peers in the upper-middle class, they receive and are able to accept high levels of human, cultural, and economic capital.[50]

Identities

The second key to understanding who falls and how relates to identities. Just as each upper-middle-class youth has a set of inherited resources, each upper-middle-class youth has an identity. Identities are senses of who we are and who we are becoming. They are multifaceted, but part of our identity relates to the roles we strive to obtain. As we repeatedly strive to obtain a particular role, we act in certain ways. Over time, vying for the same goal and acting in the same ways makes us feel like a certain type of person—someone who not only wants a particular role but who is partly defined by the role and the attempt to obtain it.[51] Many different people work toward the same goal and therefore come to feel like the same type of person. These parts of our identities are then widely shared and recognizable to others. In fact, they are so widely known that they are popularly represented as archetypes:

- The professional: college-educated worker
- The stay-at-home mother: wife and mother
- The family man: husband, father, and provider
- The rebel: anti-institutional rule-breaker
- The artist: member of a creative field
- The athlete: sports-star or sports-industry worker
- The explorer: individual with multiple identities

Different upper-middle-class youth adopt different identities. As Table 1.1 displays, individuals tend to adopt identities that make a virtue of their inherited resource weaknesses.[52] To make a virtue of resource weaknesses is to reject what one's resources make difficult to attain while favoring what one's resources allow them to achieve. For example, youth who inherit relatively low levels of academic and institutional knowledge are likely to

Table 1.1 The Pushes and Pulls into Identities

Resource Weakness	Area of Struggle	Community	Corresponding Identity	How Identities Turn Struggles into Strengths
None	None	Liberal	Professional	N/A. Builds on strengths. Purpose, status, and achievements come from school and work
Human & Cultural	School & Work	Conservative	Stay-at-Home Mother	Purpose, status, and achievements come from marriage and motherhood, not school and work
None or Human & Cultural	School & Work	Conservative	Family Man	Purpose, status, and achievements come from marriage, fatherhood, and being a provider, not high levels of success in school and work
Human & Cultural	School & Work	Liberal	Rebel	Purpose, status, and achievements come from independence, not high levels of success in any institution
Economic	Status via Money	Either	Artist or Athlete	Purpose, status, and achievements come from pursuing passions, not money
None, All, or Any	None or Any	Either	Explorer	Purpose, status, and achievements come from pursuing many forms of success rather than one

Note: These resource-community-identity combinations reflect those most often in the data rather than a list of every possible combination.

struggle in school, college, and professional work. They are then unlikely to identify as professionals—an identity that is easier to enact with high levels of academic and institutional knowledge. However, low levels of academic and institutional knowledge will not prevent them from marrying, becoming a parent, or achieving independence. They will gravitate toward identities that highlight these achievements—identities such as the stay-at-home mother, family man, and rebel. Upper-middle-class youth who inherit relatively little money make a virtue of their resource weaknesses too. They tend to avoid identities that require economic resources to enact and adopt identities that cast their resource weakness in a positive light. They identify as artists or athletes—identities that suggest pursuing a passion is more important than pursuing or possessing money. In short, youth reject identities that they lack the resources to enact and adopt identities that define the most important accomplishments as the ones their inherited resources equip them to achieve.

At times, there are multiple identities that fit youth's resource profile. Which identity youth adopt is typically narrowed by their community.[53] There are two relevant types of communities: liberal and conservative. Liberal communities—ones often located in secular spaces in cities and along coastlines—typically push women and men to invest in work before marriage, in order and importance.[54] Conservative communities—ones often located in right-wing religious areas and in smaller communities away from the coasts—more often push women and men to put marriage before work, in order and importance.[55] Most identity archetypes contain an ordering and priority of work versus marriage, and youth tend to gravitate toward the identity that is given the most status in their community. And, of course, communities that push youth toward particular identities may give them the resources—and only the resources—they need to achieve them.[56] Thus, as Table 1.1 and Appendix Table A.3 display, all youth do not hold equal likelihoods of adopting each identity. Instead, youth tend to adopt the identity that their resources allow and their community rewards.

How Inherited Resources and Identities Relate to Downward Mobility

Both inherited resources and identities relate to mobility paths.

Youth's inherited resources place them on a mobility track. Youth with inherited resource strengths tend to enter class reproduction tracks. Youth with inherited resource weaknesses tend to enter downwardly mobile ones.[57]

Of course, an explanation of downward mobility based on inherited resources alone only takes us so far. In upper-middle-class communities, youth who receive relatively few resources from their parents can acquire them from other sources. Teachers, friends, friends' parents, parents' friends, coaches, neighbors, religious congregants, and the Internet are available to upper-middle-class youth who want to build their academic skills and institutional knowledge. In addition, youth raised with relatively little money can use their institutional knowledge to access more or strategize to stay in the upper-middle-class without it.[58] An explanation of downward mobility from the upper-middle class must account for why youth with inherited resource weaknesses do not overcome them.

Identities answer this question. *Inherited resources* (resources parents pass down and children accept) tend to lead to identities, and, once identities are formed, they direct what *acquired resources* (resources youth gain on their own) youth try to obtain.[59] Youth who inherit relatively low levels of resources tend to adopt identities that make a virtue of their resource weaknesses. They then cast their resource weaknesses in a positive light rather than trying to acquire resource strengths; they also disinvest in the institutions that reward the resource strengths they do not possess. Enacting identities that encourage maintaining resource weaknesses typically means remaining on downwardly mobile trajectories—without more resources, youth have difficulty switching tracks. Thus, as Figure 1.1 shows, inherited resources typically place youth on a mobility trajectory and identities glue them to it.

We can then answer the question of who falls and how. Inherited resources and identities answer the who question—youth with inherited resource weaknesses and identities that reinforce them are most likely to fall. Identities answer the how question too—youth fall by internalizing identities that lead them to maintain resource weaknesses rather than turning them into resource strengths. We can also see this by focusing on each identity and its relationship to inherited resources, acquired resources, and downward mobility—starting with the professional.

The Professional
Youth who identify as professionals tend to grow up with resource strengths: high levels of economic capital, as reflected by their parents'

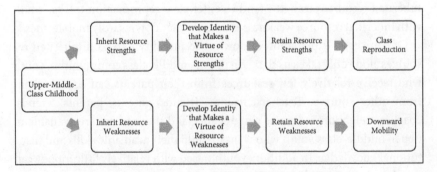

Figure 1.1 Typical Class Trajectories of Children Born into the Upper-Middle Class

earnings, and high levels of human and cultural capital, as reflected by having at least one hands-on, college-educated professional parent. They also tend to live in liberal areas, ones that push women and men to invest in work before marriage, both in order and importance.[60] The professional identity is one in which youth tie their identities to achieving in school, college, and professional work. Enacting their identity, they spend much of their time on schoolwork, acquire additional knowledge about how to navigate the institutions they are in, and stay focused on finding and then engaging in professional jobs. Doing so preserves their high levels of resource strengths and enables them to reproduce their class position.

The Stay-at-Home Mom

The 1950s popularized the idea of the stay-at-home mother,[61] and the idea of women devoting their lives to their spouse and children is still with us.[62] The stay-at-home mom identity is held by women who prioritize marriage and motherhood to the exclusion of professional work—not women who plan to punctuate their careers with a few years at home.

The stay-at-home mother identity tends to be adopted by women who grow up with little human and cultural capital compared with peers in their social class. This group tends to have mothers who have relatively low levels of education and professional workforce participation and fathers who are hands-off, college-educated professionals. The parent who spends the most time with them, the mother, is ill-prepared to provide them with high levels of academic skills and institutional know-how and the parent who is well-prepared to do so, the father, is too hands-off to do so. These women also tend to grow up with stay-at-home mothers who are valued members of their families and in conservative communities that celebrate family before work. Their resources weaknesses then push them away from identifying with school, college, and professional work, while their communities pull them toward identifying with marriage and motherhood. They do so—learning to see themselves as stay-at-home moms.

The stay-at-home mother identity makes a virtue of women's resource weaknesses—a process that makes it difficult for many to stay in the upper-middle class. Those with college-educated mothers tend to inherit just enough academic and institutional knowledge to graduate from college and meet and marry a college-educated professional—reproducing their class position. Those without college-educated mothers inherit even less academic and institutional knowledge—making college difficult for them. Seeing their purpose as about marriage and motherhood rather than about school, college, and professional work, they do not acquire the additional resources they would need to graduate from a four-year college. Not in college, they meet and marry men without college degrees. They do not complete college nor find professional jobs, and neither do their husbands. Their marriages reinforce the downwardly mobile pathway their resources put them on.

The Family Man

The 1950s also popularized the image of the family man—the married father who works to support his family but whose heart belongs at home.[63] Two types of men tend to adopt the family man identity. The first group are men raised in conservative communities with resource strengths. These men are inspired by their communities' celebration of marriage and fatherhood and want to be the type of man their communities reward. The second group are men raised in conservative communities with relatively little human and cultural capital. For them, the family man identity is not only celebrated by their communities but also allows them to gain status with the resources they are given. The identity downplays the achievements their inherited resources deny them—high levels of success in school and work—and plays up the achievements they are likely to obtain: marriage, fatherhood, and serving as a family-focused provider.

Of course, identities that make a virtue of inherited resource weaknesses do not encourage men to overcome them. Thus, despite growing up in resource-rich communities, family men whose parents give them little academic and institutional knowledge see little reason to acquire more. Their identities are built upon throwing themselves into family more than work, and they can become providers without college degrees or professional jobs. Without a reason to turn their inherited resource weaknesses into acquired resource strengths, these men embark on downwardly mobile paths. Family men whose parents offer them more resources also see little reason to invest heavily in school or work. Yet, having inherited resource strengths, they could minimally invest in maintaining them and remain on the edge of the upper-middle class. In fact, while some family men enter downwardly mobile tracks, many others enter tenuous class reproduction ones.

The Rebel

The archetype of the rebel is someone who breaks rules, revels in their own freedom and pleasure, and openly rejects their parents and institutions.

Primarily men, they are raised in liberal communities—those that reject early marriage—and without a college-educated professional parent who actively passes down academic and institutional knowledge. These youth have few options to gain worth as marriage is unavailable to them as a high-status option, and they lack the inherited resources to stand out in school, college, and professional work. They rebel, rejecting the institutions that would likely reject them. Doing so fulfills their identities as rebels but demotivates them to acquire the resources they need to stay in the upper-middle class. Most do not acquire these resources and fall into downwardly mobile trajectories.

Artists and Athletes

Artist and athlete identities are adopted by youth in either liberal or conservative communities whose parents pass down relatively low levels of economic resources. Artists and athletes make a virtue of their limited economic resources; the archetype of the authentic artist and the authentic athlete is one who pursues their craft or sport for personal fulfillment rather than economic gain. Their downplaying of money maintains their artistic and athletic identities but simultaneously keeps them on track for downward mobility. Without thinking about making money, they do not realize that there are few full-time and steady jobs that match their passions or that the existing ones are difficult to obtain. Most do not receive these jobs, leaving them poised for downward mobility.

Explorers

The model of the explorer is a well-rounded person who would rather have multiple experiences and identities than settle for one. There are several types of explorers, but they have one thing in common: their inherited resources and communities pull them toward different identities. For example, women raised by hands-on professional parents in conservative communities want to become professionals—which they have the resources to do—and stay-at-home mothers, which their communities celebrate. Women raised by moderately hands-off professional parents in liberal communities receive enough resources to flirt with becoming a professional while also missing enough resources that they feel drawn to identities that make a virtue of resource weaknesses: the artist, rebel, and sometimes the stay-at-home mother too. Men with relatively low levels of economic resources often want to be artists but some in conservative communities feel pressured to become family men and some in liberal communities feel pressured to become professionals. All of these groups bounce back and forth between identities. Doing so makes it difficult to steadfastly acquire resources related to becoming a college-educated professional or marrying one. With the exception of women who identify as both professionals and stay-at-home mothers, most explorers do not acquire the resources related to staying in their class. Instead, they enter downwardly mobile trajectories.

Exceptions

Not all youth internalize identities that match their resource profile. Unlike explorers who hold multiple identities at once, some youth hold a single identity that their resources and communities do not predict. These youth identify as professionals despite growing up with resource weaknesses or identify as stay-at-home mothers, rebels, artists, or athletes despite growing up with resource strengths. These exceptional cases show that mobility pathways are driven by inherited resources among youth with the same identities just as mobility pathways are steered by identities among youth with the same inherited resources. In other words, these exceptional cases affirm that both resources and identities matter for mobility.

There are also youth whose experiences are exceptional in a different way: their inherited resources or identities change. Both are unusual for white upper-middle-class youth. Generally, this group experiences stable resources and communities,[64] and as identities follow from resources and communities, they usually hold stable identities too. Moreover, early identities propel their continuation as they lead individuals to interpret their environment through them, select settings that reinforce them, and remind themselves that they are certain types of people.[65] Yet, changes do happen in youth's inherited resources and identities—even if only occasionally. When youth's inherited resources change, their identities often do too, and then their mobility pathways change as well. When youth's inherited resources remain stable but their identities change, their mobility pathways change too. These cases reinforce that to understand who falls and how, we need to understand both inherited resources and identities.

Why They Don't See It Coming

Why do youth who inherit resource weaknesses and form identities that maintain them not anticipate their downward mobility and change course? For some, the reason is simple: they recognize that their goals conflict with class reproduction and choose to pursue their goals. Others, however, are surprised by their impending downward mobility. Two factors mask the connection between resources, identity, and downward mobility, giving some youth a false sense that they can enact their identities and maintain their class position.[66]

The first masking mechanism is *generational change*. Generational change refers to situations in which children need more resources than their parents to enter the upper-middle class. Generational change sparks surprise as youth match their parents' resources and identities but find themselves unable to maintain their parents' class position. Generational change happens for stay-at-home mothers and family men, both of whom need more human and cultural capital than their parents to remain in their class. Stay-at-home mothers are blinded by the changed marriage market— one that makes human and cultural capital more central to marrying into the upper-middle class currently than it did for their mothers. Family men are blinded by the changed labor market—one that makes human and cultural capital more central to finding a professional job for themselves than their fathers.

The second masking mechanism is *life course change*. Life course change refers to instances when resources and identities move youth toward class reproduction early in their lives but away from it as they age. Most youth who experience life course change do not realize that their resources and identities are liabilities for their class position until their downward trajectory has begun; they then feel betrayed by the sudden bait and switch. For example, schools tolerate rebels' low levels of resources, rule breaking, and anti-authority stance. Colleges allow them as well. Schools and colleges are associated with moving upper-middle-class youth toward class reproduction, and rebels learn that they can enact their identity and stay on a class reproduction track. However, professional employers have no reason to hire young adults who break rules, challenge authority, and have relatively little academic knowledge. Rebels' identities then suddenly become at odds with the institutions that can keep them in the upper-middle class—an abrupt switch that counters the message they learned in school and college. The shifting value of what resources and identities are needed to avoid downward mobility—both between generations and within them—makes it difficult for youth to anticipate their class trajectory.

The Consequences

The rise of social class inequality spread fear that our class system now locks upper-middle-class youth in their class of birth while locking everyone else out. Understanding who falls and how reveals that these fears are both overstated and not nearly serious enough. They are overstated in that there is one Vera for every Julie—one person leaves the upper-middle class for every person who remains.[67] But these fears are understated too. While upper-middle-class youth do not have a lock on upper-middle-class adulthoods, if the youth in this study are any indication, those raised with resource strengths and professional identities nearly do. Thus, downward mobility does not show that the class structure is open, fair, or meritocratic. Instead, even among youth born near the top, where and with what they are raised relates to where and with what they end up.

Moreover, downward mobility shows the rigidity of the class system in that even those who fall do not become disadvantaged—at least not in early adulthood and not when compared with their peers who were born into lower classes. Upper-middle-class youth raised with economic resource weaknesses and with identities that maintained them tended to graduate from a four-year college—receiving a degree that only one in three Americans obtain.[68] Upper-middle-class youth raised with human and cultural resource weaknesses and identities that maintained them less often graduated from college, found professional jobs, or married college-educated professionals. This put them in the company of most Americans—not at the bottom of the class structure.[69] Thus, while the class structure is more open when youth like Vera fall than when they do not, downward mobility still highlights the rigidity of the class system. Only the privileged section of a privileged class avoid it, and those who fall rarely fall far.[70]

Outline of the Book

The remainder of the book describes who is poised for downward mobility, how they fall, and why not all of them see it coming. Each of the next six chapters focus on three respondents who are exemplars of their identity group. However, they are not the only ones with their resources, identities, and mobility trajectories or the only ones who experience masking mechanisms. Table A.4 in the appendix lists the number of respondents in each group and the percentage who are downwardly mobile.

The chapters proceed as follows. Chapter 2 begins with the professionals and their class reproduction trajectory. Chapters 3–5 focus on youth who inherit limited amounts of academic and institutional knowledge, and how the stay-at-home mother, family man, and rebel identities, respectively, relate to their mobility trajectory. Chapter 6 focuses on youth who inherit limited economic capital—artists and athletes—and their path to college and nonprofessional jobs. Chapter 7 discusses how explorers' identities relate to their pathways toward class reproduction and downward mobility. Chapter 8 documents the exceptions and how their cases show that both resource inheritances and identities relate to downward mobility. Chapter 9 concludes the book with a discussion of the implications of this new view of downward mobility. Finally, the methodological appendix provides more information on the data and how I analyzed it, and the tables appendix provides support for the claims in the book. The theoretical appendix presents the book's contributions in more sociological terms—detailing how the book revises Bourdieu's idea of the habitus to account for downward mobility.

Overall, this book tells the stories of the downwardly mobile—of who falls, how they fall, and why they do not see it coming. First, however, it turns to more familiar stories—the stories of how the privileged stay privileged.

2

Professionals

Nancy, Molly, and Bert had it all.

Nancy was a gregarious teen with long blonde hair and hazel eyes that she swore Joe Biden once complimented. The daughter of a financial manager and a stay-at-home mom, her father's income allowed her to grow up in a large house in a coastal suburb and his hands-on parenting style and graduate school education gave her a live-in tutor and academic coach. Fortified with the resources she needed to become a professional, she set her sights on that goal from an early age. At just 13 years old, with a whiff of whimsy and precocity, Nancy held childhood dreams while also imagining herself destined for a future as a professional: "Hopefully I'll be a movie star, and if I do become a movie star, I'm not gonna be like one of those bimbos without a college degree. I'm gonna have a college degree and possibly a PhD, that's what my dad wants. And then I'm gonna use my fame to get some ideas across to people. And if I don't become that, I'm gonna be a teacher, 'cause I think we need to start to educate our youth." By age 15, Nancy had given up her ideas of becoming a movie star to concentrate on becoming a college-educated professional. Now, she said, she would change lives by becoming a public schoolteacher at a Title I school.

Molly had it all too. The daughter of professionals, she grew up in what her interviewer called a mecca of wealth and wore clothes that gave her a glamorous appearance. Though both of her parents had high levels of economic, human, and cultural capital, it was her mother who made it her mission to pass down her academic skills and institutional know-how to Molly. In a liberal community,[1] Molly's mother taught her academic lessons and informed her that community colleges, four-year colleges, and graduate schools' regular procedures could be modified to admit young and ambitious students. As a teen, Molly inhabited the identity that was allowed and encouraged given the resources she inherited—she defined herself as a budding professional. At age 16, she was eager to start professional work even if it meant rushing through her college years: "It would be nice to finish college, but finishing college for me is just another step to

Privilege Lost. Jessi Streib, Oxford University Press (2020) © Oxford University Press.
DOI: 10.1093/oso/9780190854041.001.0001

get into a good graduate school program, so if I could just get into a good graduate school program [without finishing college], I could start doing my thing two years earlier." Dreaming of becoming a professional, it could not come too soon.

Bert grew up similarly privileged—even among youth of his social class. His father earned a graduate degree from a prestigious university and worked as a business executive; his mother earned a master's degree from the same prestigious university and was employed as a social worker. Bert's parents shared their resources with him—using them to live in a liberal suburb known for its strong public schools, to help him select courses and earn high grades, and to build his skills through at-home academic lessons and debates. At age 14, Bert, a tall and thin teen with dark hair that some-times drooped over his eyes, imagined the future his inherited resources would allow. Without knowing the specifics, he knew he wanted to become a professional: "I want to have a successful job and just do well in school and go to college."

Nancy, Molly, and Bert shared similar resources, grew up in similar communities—liberal ones—and held similar ideas of who they would be-come: professionals.[2] Nancy would embrace higher education and become a teacher; Molly would attend graduate school and obtain a job that required it; and Bert would have a "successful job." These identities reflected their high levels of inherited resources and their communities' ideas of who they should become. They would also tie them to the track their resources placed them upon—one toward class reproduction.

Resources, Communities, and the Professional Identity

There is a common image of the professional—one portrayed in the media but also passed down through stories parents tell their children.[3] The profes-sional is presented as a well-paid and respected individual who does intrinsi-cally interesting and important work. The people who become professionals are smart and hardworking; with costly barriers to entry, they are the only people said to succeed. Professionals also work long hours[4]—partly because they are salaried and expected to keep working until the job is done—but also because they love the work and desire a sense of achievement.[5] Their jobs are their passions and their main source of meaning. They want to dedi-cate their lives to their careers.

The idea of the professional is esteemed in liberal upper-middle-class communities. In these places, children are often socialized to become professionals from young ages. Parents pour over child development books to learn how to intellectually stimulate their infants, encourage their toddlers to use their words, teach their young children to conflate fun with intellectual work, and send their children to preschools that promise to prepare them for college.[6]

As children grow, upper-middle-class parents in liberal communities continue to push the professional identity. They often model the importance of school by monitoring their children's schoolwork, fighting for their children to be placed in higher academic tracks or with better teachers, and enrolling their children in the multimillion dollar industry of test-prep, tutoring, and academic camps.[7] They also repeatedly talk to their children about college and periodically check what work their children want to do when they grow up—reminding their children that college is part of their future and that work is central to who they will become.[8] Their children notice the emphasis their parents place on academic success and the future they say it will bring. Many upper-middle-class children in liberal communities internalize that schoolwork, college, and professional work should be central to them, too. Indeed, not all even realize there are other options. Attending college and entering the professional workforce is the only future many youth imagine.[9]

Meanwhile, in these same upper-middle-class liberal communities, romantic relationships do not receive as much of parents' attention or effort.[10] To the extent that parents involve themselves in their children's romantic lives, it is to ensure that their relationships do not interfere with their children's future careers. Liberal upper-middle-class parents typically confirm that their children are informed about sex and have access to contraception; they want to ensure that an accidental pregnancy does not derail their child's occupational opportunities. They also monitor their children's romantic relationships to make certain that they do not become so consuming that their professional prospects suffer.[11] The message children receive is then loud and clear: their parents' intensity about school and work communicates that it should be central to their identities, and their parents' framing of romantic relationships as a potential threat to their futures tells them that it should not be at their core.

Of course, not everyone can successfully enact a professional identity. To successfully act as a high-achieving and smart person, youth must have others recognize them as high-achieving and smart too. Doing so is most accessible to youth raised with high levels of human, cultural, and economic capital—even compared with those in their social class.[12] Institutions reward what they do not teach: schools, colleges, and workplaces determine who is talented, smart, and high-achieving largely based upon the academic skills youth are taught at home, the institutional know-how that allows them to do what is expected but unsaid, and the money to attend the schools and build the résumés that are deemed the most meritorious.[13]

Upper-middle-class youth who identify as professionals tend to have parents who are prepared and able to give them these resources. They have at least one parent who is a college-educated professional and who actively teaches them academic and cultural skills. Nancy's, Molly's, and Bert's parents were no exception in this regard, with Molly's parents being the most intense. Molly's graduate-school-educated mother monitored Molly's homework and taught Molly over the summer so she could gain an academic headstart. Molly's mother then pushed Molly to enroll in college while her peers were still in high school and remained by Molly's side through the process. She volunteered to take college classes with Molly to help her with homework; she also lived with Molly during her college years so that she could offer academic support. Molly's father helped her too; Molly credited him with a high grade in one of her college classes—a class she thought she would fail without his academic assistance.

Nancy's and Bert's parents were not as intense, but Nancy and Bert still reported learning academic skills from them. At age 15 Nancy said her dad "does everyone's homework," and at age 18 Nancy still said she turned to her dad for homework help. At age 14, Bert worried that high school would bring two hours of homework each night. His mother advised him: "You better do all two hours of it," and Bert knew she would make sure he did. Nancy's and Bert's parents also taught them skills that are rewarded in school. Nancy developed her communication skills by regularly debating politics with her father, her analytical skills by dissecting old movies with him, and her literary knowledge by talking with him about famous books. Bert routinely had what he called "scholarly conversations" with his father—ones that covered philosophy, politics, and religion—and occasionally talked about these topics with his mother as well. His parents not only taught him about the content of these fields, but also modeled how to debate academic knowledge and the idea that doing so is fun.

Molly, Nancy, and Bert—like others who identified as professionals—also said their parents helped them navigate institutions. Molly's mother chose a college for her and then helped select her major. Nancy said her father gave her daily reminders that college scholarships would improve her options and were attainable if she earned high grades. Bert's mother told him about the different types of colleges, and, at age 14, Bert knew his mother hoped he would attend a liberal arts college. In addition, Molly, Nancy, and Bert each had parents who earned substantial sums of money—enough to pay to live in districts with strong schools and to participate in the extracurricular activities some associate with success. In sum, Molly, Nancy, and Bert received at home the skills that were rewarded in school, college, and work—the skills that enabled them to present themselves as professionals.

Reproducing Their Identities and Their Resources

Receiving high levels of academic skills, institutional insights, and economic resources from their parents, Nancy, Molly, and Bert came to feel like the type of person their resources allowed: professionals. They enacted this identity as they moved through school, college, work, and romantic relationships. In acting like a professional, they collected more resources and maintained their resource strengths. With these resources, they reproduced their class position.

School

The archetype of the professional is a smart worker who constantly strives for achievement, puts in long hours for the sake of intrinsically interesting and important work, and earns a paycheck.[14] As teenagers, youth could not yet access professional work, but they could treat school as professionals treat work.[15] That is, they could work long hours on schoolwork, strive for a sense of achievement, focus on being smart, frame schoolwork as intrinsically interesting, and talk of the money they would earn in the future. Doing so encouraged them to build upon their early advantages by acquiring even more academic knowledge, institutional know-how, and economic resources.

Nancy enacted the professional identity while in middle and high school. She did so by treating her academic work as if it were part of a high-powered job that required relentless hours. At age 13, Nancy pronounced: "I'm so busy most of the time with homework and stuff that I literally forget to shower sometimes. I'll go a couple of days without showering, and I don't smell myself so my mom's like, 'Nancy, take a shower!' I'm like, 'I can't! I have so much homework!'" Nancy not only spent long hours on homework but studying for standardized tests too; she began studying for the SAT a year before the exam. Like a professional, Nancy also desired concrete signs of achievement. She claimed: "I have to get a 4.0. I just have to." She received special permission to take advanced placement courses as a high school sophomore as well—acquiring another public sign of achievement.[16] In addition, Nancy saw herself as a future worker and vowed not to become like her mother who was unpaid. At age 18, she derided her mother for having a different identity: "She's your stereotypical, I don't want to say this because it sounds racist, but it's not: Jewish American Princess. She's always had everything. First it was her father, now it's her husband who she's just like, 'Okay I'm going to go out and buy something and then you'll find a way.'" To ensure she did not become her mother, Nancy talked to the adults she knew about which colleges to apply to, how to get in, and how to pay the high financial costs.

Like Nancy, Molly grew up displaying a professional identity. At age 16, Molly spent as much time on her schoolwork as powerful professionals would on paid work: "During the school year I don't go out at all. It's just schoolwork, home, schoolwork, home. That's all I do." Molly also matched the professional archetype by dedicating herself to academic achievement. Earning straight As was her primary goal; Molly was delighted when her classmates called her a genius, felt a thrill from high grades, and chastised her sister for going on an occasional date rather than completely dedicating herself to her studies. As part of enacting a professional identity, Molly also learned how to navigate school and college in ways that displayed and enabled her achievement. At age 16, she could talk about which colleges were party schools and which were for serious academics like her, and she had already researched graduate schools' admissions requirements and begun working toward them. Moreover, the archetype of a professional is of an earner, and, at age 16, Molly considered bringing home a paycheck to be an integral part of her future: "I want to be set financially set. I think that's a big goal."

Bert, too, strove to earn good grades to secure his identity as a future professional. At age 14, he said: "I think it's really important to do well because I think it's important to go to a good college, get a good job, and you need good grades in school to do that." He earned mostly As, spent hours each night on schoolwork, and announced that he enjoyed school. It was not surprising that he enjoyed school. It was a place where he could display his professional identity. Of course, by acting like professionals in school, Nancy, Molly, and Bert built on their early resource strengths.[17] Their studying and dedication to achievement increased their academic knowledge, led them to seek out institutional insights, and kept them focused on becoming an earner. The identity also prepared them for the next step on a class reproduction path: college.

College

Once in college, Nancy, Molly, and Bert continued to enact a professional identity. And, just as they gained more academic skills and institutional know-how by enacting the professional identity in high school, they did so in college too.

Nancy used her time in college to enact a tenet of the professional archetype—dedication to work. Wanting to be a teacher, Nancy became an education major, participated in an honors training program for education majors, engaged in student teaching, and took only one elective outside of her major. She also dedicated herself to navigating the labor market; she poured over school districts' employment numbers so she could focus her applications on schools that tended to hire. The professional archetype also includes financial independence, and Nancy planned to abide by this tenet too. She knew that teachers' salaries were relatively low, so she moved in with her aunt to save enough money to support herself later.

Molly also enacted a professional identity while in college. As part of her identity, she continued to treat academics as a full-time professional job. She discussed her schedule: "Monday through Friday, I do homework all the day. This coming semester, I go to school Tuesdays and Thursdays for most of the morning. The rest of days and after, I come home from school, I work out, and I do homework. I have tons of homework to do. Homework and school. Then I hang with my boyfriend one night a week, that's all I give him, that's all I have time for. So it's just homework and school." She not only worked long hours, but, like a professional, focused on achievement too. She called herself a control freak about her grades and said that earning high grades was the most exciting part of her life.

In addition, Molly used her existing knowledge about how to navigate institutions to learn more about them. She felt comfortable interacting with professors and described herself as the student who repeatedly said: "I have to make sure that I get all the information from the professor." She talked to her professors outside of class too—seeking their advice about how to prepare for graduate school and which schools to choose. The archetype of the professional is of a high earner too, and Molly continued to say that earning was important: "I think it's important to be comfortable financially. I have a tendency to want more and more money."

Bert, too, enacted a professional identity in college. At age 19, he described himself as an "intellectual" and "deep-thinker." Displaying his professional identity, he kept a shelf of textbooks over his bed and read them for fun; he even kept them there after his friends teased him about his interests. He also threw himself into his schoolwork and into preparation for his professional work: "I have to get certain grades and do really well on the MCAT and work really hard and have a lot of volunteer experience. I know it's a lot of work." He added: "I'm going to work really hard in school so I can go to med school and be successful in a career that I'm pretty sure that I'm going to love." He spent his "free time" in professors' labs and his summers working in hospitals. He also carefully researched medical schools' requirements, sought professors' advice about the best way to meet them, and looked forward to earning "real money." His way of navigating college signaled that he thought work was intrinsically interesting, that he enjoyed achieving, that he was committed to work, and that he anticipated becoming an earner—that he was a professional. Of course, enacting the professional identity helped Nancy, Molly, and Bert become one. It helped them maintain high levels of academic skills and institutional knowledge while also focusing on earning—resources and ideas that facilitated becoming professional workers.

Work

Youth with professional identities had long thrown themselves into their schoolwork; after finishing their educations they threw themselves into their paid work too. They found their work intrinsically interesting, enjoyed the sense of accomplishment work provided, and spent long hours at their jobs. At age 23, Nancy continued to enact the professional identity, talking of her job as her main source of joy and purpose. She said of teaching: "I picked something that I loved. I love going to work every day. Even with all the stupid paperwork I have to do and all this other crap, I don't care, I love it. I love my students, my job." In her mid-20s, Molly felt the same way. She found her work as a professor intrinsically interesting, saying: "I love it. It's so much fun. I love teaching . . . I love, love working on papers, and working from home, and my colleagues—it's an awesome job for me." Molly also continued to devote long hours to her work, describing herself as "definitely hard-working, workaholic tendencies maybe, but definitely hardworking." Bert, at age 24, also found his work intrinsically interesting and devoted long hours to it. He spent nearly all of his time in his MD/PhD program, nearly everyone he interacted with outside of his family was in his program, and what little free time he had he spent lobbying his state government about medical is-sues. Tying their identities to their jobs, they put their hearts and their time into them. Doing so increased the probability that they would maintain their professional position—and, by default, their class position.

Romantic Relationships

Youth with professional identities focused on school, college, and work. In throwing themselves into these institutions, they threw themselves out of the romantic and marriage markets—at least for a time. Doing so corresponded to the values of their liberal communities—ones that put work before mar-riage in order and importance.

Nancy delayed committed romantic relationships, framing them as op-posed to her identity. At age 15, she described dating another student for a year and half, but it wasn't serious. According to Nancy, he focused more on video games than on her, and they went six months without talking at all. By age 18, Nancy had tried dating again but did not see romantic relationships as related to her identity or worth taking up her time. She explained: "I'm such a busy person, I just don't have time to be chilling with you all the time." At age 23, Nancy still refrained from dating for the same reasons: "I haven't really dated that much. I'm not asexual, but, because I'm so driven, I'm al-ways so busy that it's not a priority." At age 23, Nancy was not considering marriage. However, if she ever did marry, she wanted it to be after she further established her career and to another professional—someone who would fortify her identity as a professional.

Molly, too, framed romantic relationships as incompatible with her identity and delayed them until becoming a professional. At age 16, Molly maintained: "The whole boyfriend thing, you have to call them every night, and it takes so much time. Every time I have an opportunity to go out I'm kind of like, 'No I don't want to go out with you 'cause I have to get done this for [grad] school, 'cause ten years from now, I want to remember this." At age 18, Molly felt the same way: "My longest relationship, sad to say, has been two or three weeks. Besides that, boys get in the way of school." In college, Molly started dating, but told her short-term boyfriend: "You get one night a week, that's all you get." At age 21, Molly had dated one person for nine months and felt relieved when the relationship ended. She explained: "I'm kinda anti-dating right now. I just really want to focus on my career and my PhD." In addition to delaying serious romantic relationships so that they did not interfere with her professional ambitions, Molly also actively rejected the idea that marriage could be a primary part of her identity. She relayed a story to illustrate her point:

> My cousin . . . ever since she was eighteen she's wanted to get married and she just turned thirty. And she ended up just getting married. Her life is just getting married and family, and that's completely cool, but the thing that was impressed upon me at her wedding was they said, "Jill was born to get married." And I just thought that was the saddest thing ever. This was her day; after this she doesn't need to accomplish anything else because she accomplished what she needed to do in life. And I felt so sad about that. I don't think I would ever want anybody to say that about me. That would be the worst thing possible.

Molly did not tie her identity to marriage but to work. However, once in her doctoral program, Molly gradually began to consider more serious romantic relationships. After initially turning down a date because she said, "I'm not going, I have homework to do!" Molly reconsidered. She began dating an older student in her PhD program, someone who shared her professional identity and could help her achieve her own. They wrote papers together, and, after he received a job, he convinced his employer to hire Molly too. Moreover, he did not demand she scale back her work hours—she estimated that she spent 55 to 60 hours a week on work after they married. With her new husband, Molly maintained her professional identity and married a professional too.

Bert's identity as a professional also meant that he delayed romantic relationships.[18] He avoided both romantic relationships and hook-ups as he believed they detracted from school and work. At age 19, he maintained: "It's not something that's a high priority right now. I'm in college now and I need to move on in school and that's something that will distract me." However, once he was in medical school and closer to reaching his professional goals, Bert started to think about marriage. Given that the only people he met were medical students, the chances he would marry another professional was high. Marriage to another professional would be fitting, as he now was a professional himself.

The Professional Identity and Class Reproduction

Nancy, Molly, and Bert had it all. They inherited high levels of economic, human, and cultural capital—even relative to their peers who were also born into the upper-middle class. They then developed identities that reflected these resource strengths and maintained them. With consistently high levels of the resources that schools, colleges, and professional workplaces reward, they sailed through each institution and onto class reproduction. They also delayed marriage until they were surrounded by other professionals, making it likely that they would reinforce their class position through marriage too.

Thus, with identities that reflected their inherited resources and that encouraged them to acquire more resources, professionals like Nancy, Molly, and Bert were on pathways to remain in the upper-middle class. Nancy became a college-educated teacher and only considered marrying another professional. Molly became a professor with a PhD and married another professor with a PhD. Bert became a medical student and prepared for a career as a surgeon or medical researcher. He, too, would likely marry another professional. As young professionals, they never left the upper-middle class.

Moving Forward

The study ended when Nancy, Molly, and Bert were in their mid-20s. We cannot know what pathway they will take as they grow older, but it is likely that they will remain in the upper-middle class. Their college degrees can never be taken away, their academic talent and institutional know-how will continue to allow them to perform professional work, and, for some, their long-held identities will keep them devoted to their jobs. Nancy predicted that she would be dedicated to her work for years to come—most likely as a teacher, though possibly as a lawyer. Molly hoped to receive tenure and hold a professional job for life. Bert thought he would become a medical professional then shift from identifying as a professional to identifying as a family man.[19] If he did, his class position, like Nancy's and Molly's, would remain secure. Decades of living-to-work would allow him to work-to-live while remaining a college-educated professional—a member of the upper-middle class.

Of course, not all youth grew up wanting to become professionals or were raised with the resources to do so. Yet, while other resource inheritances and identities would provide status and a sense of satisfaction, no other set would be so associated with class reproduction. This was certainly true for upper-middle-class youth in the next chapter.

3

Stay-at-Home Mothers

Not everyone born into the upper-middle class has it all.

Virginia did not have it all—though from the outside it appeared that she did. Virginia was an assertive and attractive woman with an athletic build, fashionable clothes, and expensive sunglasses. Her father was a prominent, college-educated businessman who grew up in a conservative religion. His six-figure income paid for Virginia, her stay-at-home mother, and her four siblings to live in a six-bedroom house in their rural red state.[1] But while Virginia grew up in a well-off family, she did not inherit each of the resources that help upper-middle-class youth stay in their original social class. Virginia described her relationship with her father as distant—as "two ships passing in the night"—and said that she had sufficiently little interaction with him that "I wouldn't know what to talk to him about." Virginia was far closer to her mother—calling herself "in her back pocket" and naming her mother as her best friend. But Virginia's mother never finished college or worked in a professional job. She wasn't well positioned to provide Virginia with high levels of two resources that would help her stay in her class—academic skills and institutional knowledge. As Virginia's father was too distant to offer these resources, Virginia was raised with little of them—at least compared with people in her class.

Sarah did not have it all either. She was a petite woman with fashionable clothes, long brown hair, carefully painted fingernails, and pearl earrings. A Mormon, Sarah was raised in a household and community with a conservative view of family—one with strict gender roles where mothers served as the primary parent. Sarah said she spent a lot of time with her mother and talked to her about everything—though everything seemed to mean romantic relationships more than school, not that it was likely to matter. Even if they had talked about school, Sarah's mother, a stay-at-home mom who had not attended a four-year college, was not well positioned to teach Sarah advanced academic skills or how to use school to prepare for college. Sarah's father, a professional in an educational setting, was prepared to do so, but Sarah never mentioned that he did. In their conservative household, marriage and family came before school and work.

Privilege Lost. Jessi Streib, Oxford University Press (2020) © Oxford University Press.
DOI: 10.1093/oso/9780190854041.001.0001

Rebecca's story was similar. Rebecca was a stylish, thin, made-up young woman who wore enough jewelry to her interviews that multiple researchers commented upon it. From the outside, she, too, looked like she had it all. Her father worked in professional sales and earned a six-figure income, allowing Rebecca to grow up in an affluent area, attend private school, travel, play tennis, frequent a country club, and be raised by a mother who did not work for pay. Her interviewer thought of Rebecca as having it all too; she wrote that Rebecca, who grew up in the Deep South, came across as a privileged southern belle. But, of course, Rebecca didn't have it all. She was close to her college-educated professional father,[2] but said he comforted her about school more than he instructed her how to succeed in it. She talked more with her mother, who pushed Rebecca to excel in school. But her push was mostly an effort to convince Rebecca to focus on school; Rebecca did not say that her stay-at-home, nonprofessional mother offered her concrete academic skills or knowledge of how schools and colleges worked.[3] However, Rebecca's mother was different in a way that would matter—though she had never been a professional, she did earn a college degree and steered Rebecca toward attending college herself.

Raised by stay-at-home mothers they admired, in variants of conservative communities—rural states, religious congregations, and the Deep South—and in upper-middle-class families that did little to transfer academic and institutional knowledge to them, Virginia, Sarah, and Rebecca came to identify as the same type of person. Virginia stated: "I always knew that I wanted to be a wife and a mother." Sarah shared: "I want to just put work aside and put everything towards my kids and just be a mom." Rebecca reported her most important goal: "To have a family and to be a good parent." As we will see, this identity celebrated the accomplishments their inherited resources allowed and their communities cherished; it also downplayed the accomplishments their inherited resources made difficult to achieve. Of course, it also gave these women a reason not to acquire the resources they did not receive—resources that help upper-middle-class youth avoid downward mobility.

Resources, Communities, and the Stay-at-Home Mother Identity

In the 1950s, a stay-at-home mother was the main role available to white women born in the upper-middle-class. An identity as a professional was denied to many women as colleges regularly capped the number of women they enrolled or closed their doors to women entirely. In the 1950s, the University of Virginia, for example, returned applications from women with the words "women need not apply," and, in the late 1960s, public universities in the state of Virginia denied admission to 21,000 women but not a single man.[4] Many employers, too, refused to hire women. In the decades before the 1950s, 75% of local school boards and 50% of business offices banned married women from working in their schools and businesses.[5] Though official marriage bars diminished in the 1950s, hiring discrimination was still legal until the passage of the Civil Rights Act of 1964 and women could be legally fired for becoming pregnant until 1978, when the Pregnancy Discrimination Act passed.[6] Moreover, in the early 1970s, landlords and banks legally discriminated against women, making it difficult for them to rent their own apartment, buy their own house, or start their own business.[7] With few options to earn their own money as a professional or to live apart from a man, many women focused on becoming a wife and mother. Women tended to marry young, moving from family to family with little in-between.[8]

Of course, more opportunities opened up to women as time went on, and women hurried to take advantage of them. The 1972 passage of Title IX prevented colleges from legally discriminating against women, and just over a decade after it passed women outnumbered men on college campuses.[9] Shortly before, private employers lost the law's permission to deny jobs to women, and women plowed into the workforce. While in 1970, only about 45% of women worked, a decade later 60% of women worked, and after more time passed, about 70% of women joined the labor force.[10]

Still, though new opportunities were open to women, not all women wanted them—nor did all Americans think it was wise for women to take them. Indeed, three decades after employment discrimination against women was outlawed, the majority of American women still considered a housewife to be a fulfilling role.[11] Around the same time, the share of women who worked full-time and wished to reduce their hours was greater than the share of stay-at-home mothers who wanted to work.[12] And, between 1994 and 2004, in the time when youth like Virginia, Sarah, and Rebecca grew up, the percent of Americans who preferred to live in a family with a breadwinning husband and stay-at-home wife increased—moving from 34% to 40%.[13] The pulls and pushes regarding becoming a stay-at-home mom were also apparent in what women passed up to do it: more than one million dollars in lifetime earnings.[14]

Both cultural and institutional factors continue to allow and encourage women to remain out of the workforce. In conservative communities, especially, gender norms remain rigid. Women have new workforce opportunities, but many conservative women see themselves as caregivers and argue that it is better for everyone—their husbands, their children, and themselves—if they remain at home.[15] Many men do little to dissuade women of this belief. Men tend to consider their own work compulsory, giving them little incentive to scale back their careers and become the primary parent.[16]

The stay-at-home mother identity is also bolstered by religious institutions. In the 1950s, conservative Christian religions aligned their teachings and infrastructure with the newly celebrated family form—the breadwinning father and stay-at-home mother.[17] They preached that men and women were fundamentally different and should take up different roles. Women, born to be nurturers, should become stay-at-home mothers when economically possible, while men, born to be leaders and managers, should take primary responsibility over the family's material needs.[18] Though these churches' proclamations loosened over time to make room for the possibility of women working and men being valued for non-economic reasons, the idea that women should become stay-at-home mothers remains a central part of their teachings.[19]

Conservative religions also reinforce the stay-at-home mother identity through their organizational practices. Gender-segregated prayer groups, youth groups, and leadership opportunities reinforce the message that men and women are different and should take different roles. At the same time, religious organizations provide space and encouragement for men and women to meet and marry. Evangelical churches and Mormon wards allow people of the same age to meet others of their faith, religious colleges bring together youth of the same religion and promote the idea of college as a marriage market, and proscriptions against premarital sex encourage early marriage. Such institutional features bolster the stay-at-home wife role; early marriage enables women to go from being supported by their parents to being supported by their husbands without needing to financially support themselves in-between.[20]

Of course, women are not only exposed to the stay-at-home mother archetype in the wider society but at home too. In the 1980s, when women like Virginia, Sarah, and Rebecca were children, over 30% of American youth were raised with a breadwinning father and stay-at-home mother.[21] Many of these families, of course, model the pull of the stay-at-home mother identity—that it is recognized and valued. In addition, they tend to give their children fewer resources than other family types, pushing their daughters into the stay-at-home mother identity too. The stay-at-home mother/breadwinning father model is based on the idea that the parent with less workforce experience—and, sometimes, less education, too—spends more time with their children than the parent whose job and education provides them with more academic skills and institutional knowledge. The resources that the family holds then are not passed down to the child, as the parent whose resources are typical of the upper-middle-class does not spend substantial time with the child, while the parent with resources more typical of the working-class does more to raise the child.[22] This issue is pronounced when mothers are not college-educated professionals before having children—something that happens more often in conservative communities than liberal ones.[23] Of course, it is also in conservative communities that parents' goal is less to turn their children into college-educated professionals than to turn them into devoted family members and religious observers—a task that requires passing down fewer academic and institutional resources.[24]

Virginia was raised in such a family and in a conservative space—in a variety of red states and by secular parents who spent their formative years as members of conservative religions. Her father earned a high income, but from Virginia's perspective, he was rarely home. When he was home, Virginia tried to learn about the workforce from him, but he did not engage. Virginia explained: "I really wish that he was more vocal, that he would talk about more things. 'Cause I know that sometimes work is really hard for him, and in my opinion he'd feel better if he talked about it . . . I feel like our relationship would be better if he trusted me to talk to me about that stuff or thought that I would get it." Virginia was much closer to her mother, but she could not play this role in Virginia's life. Having dropped out of college to become a stay-at-home mom, Virginia's mother never entered the professional workforce or gained the knowledge associated with it.

Sarah also grew up in a family with a stay-at-home mother who had not graduated from a four-year college and with a breadwinning father who financially supported them. Her father, a graduate-school-educated professional, likely had knowledge of how schools, colleges, and workplaces operated, as well as the academic abilities to succeed in them. However, Sarah did not report talking to him about it.[25] There was little reason for Sarah to seek his advice or for him to offer it. Raised a Mormon, Sarah learned that she need not concern herself with the path to professional work. The church's *Eternal Marriage Student Manual* proclaimed: "No career approaches in importance that of wife, homemaker, mother—cooking meals, washing dishes, making beds for one's precious husband and children." It also explicitly stated that women should not identify as professionals: "It is folly to neglect [marriage] preparation for education in unrelated fields just to prepare temporarily to earn money. Women, when you are married it is the husband's role to provide, not yours."[26] Sarah understood what was expected of her. She revealed: "In the religion that I am, being a Mormon, there's just so much pressure to get married and start a family." She was not upset that her family did not provide her with an academic headstart or substantial institutional knowledge. Like Virginia, she admired the role her mother played and felt little pressure to find professional work or to acquire the resources to do so.

Rebecca also grew up in a conservative social space. Though she was not particularly religious, she felt that her regional community upheld conservative gender roles. Asked why she wanted to marry, Rebecca stated: "I think a lot of it is our culture, especially in the South. A lot of girls are twenty years old and have a boyfriend and want to get married right out of college."[27] Rebecca, like Virginia and Sarah, was also raised by a stay-at-home mother and working father and also said she spent more time with her mother than her father. However, unlike Virginia's and Sarah's mothers, Rebecca's mother had a four-year college degree. Rebecca claimed her mother pushed her to earn higher grades, and Rebecca grew up assuming she would attend college. Having married into money herself, Rebecca's mother also gave her advice about how to do the same. Rebecca relayed: "My mom has always said . . . there are nice guys and there are nice guys that have a lot of money, too."

Thus, Virginia, Sarah, and Rebecca were all pushed and pulled into a stay-at-home mother identity. These identities were honored in their families, celebrated in their communities, and made a virtue of their inherited resource weakness. They could give little credence to the institutions that required human and cultural capital to succeed and focus on marriage and motherhood instead—institutions in which these resources were needed less. Yet, while focusing on marriage and motherhood would be consistent with their identities, it would not keep all of them in their class. Stay-at-home mothers with little human and cultural capital regularly entered downwardly mobile trajectories.

Reproducing Their Identities and Their Resources

It takes resources to stay in the upper-middle-class. Schools, colleges, and workplaces promote youth with academic skills and institutional knowledge, and—as we will see later—marriage to a professional is now eased by possessing these resources too. Girls and women who identified as stay-at-home mothers did not inherit high levels of these resources. They then engaged in school, college, work, and marriage in ways that expressed their identities but did not turn their resource weaknesses into resource strengths. For those who inherited the least resources, this approach would cost them their class position.

School

Not all youth focus on the school's official mission—to teach academics—or revolve their lives around earning high grades. Women who identified as stay-at-home mothers navigated school in ways aligned with their identities. As unmarried teens, they were not yet stay-at-home mothers, but they could still act in ways aligned with the identity—they could focus on romance and distance themselves from the work that schools assigned. They approached school as a romantic zone, a place where they could meet and interact with boyfriends, and as a holding zone, a place to pass through before they could get on with their lives. They then hoped for high grades but put little effort into obtaining them.[28] This approach shored up their identities but did not encourage them to acquire high levels of the resources their parents had not passed down—academic skills and institutional knowledge.

Virginia, for example, did not use school to prepare for college and work. Instead, she considered school a holding zone and a romantic zone. Regarding the former, she saw school as the process of "sitting in a classroom learning stuff I don't care about." At the same time, she met her first boyfriend in high school and enjoyed spending time with him at school. Yet, after Virginia's boyfriend slept with her best friend while Virginia was passed out, drunk, on the other side of the room, Virginia returned to seeing school as a holding zone. She skipped school when she could. She did not see the point in attending.

Rebecca, too, navigated school in a way that emphasized her identity as a stay-at-home mother. At age 16, Rebecca failed her math class. She explained that her low grade was a result of considering school a place to interact with her boyfriend rather than a place to focus on academics: "This boy that never tried grade wise, he took up all my time. Then I didn't really try in school." Sarah was not allowed to date until she was 16 years old and therefore did not begin high school thinking of it as a romantic site. Instead, she saw high school as a holding zone—a place to pass through until she could become a wife and mom. She revealed: "School's always been kinda hard for me. It's not something I've always been really motivated about." Virginia's, Sarah's, and Rebecca's approaches to school corresponded to their identities—ones in which relationships, not academics, were central to who they were and saw themselves becoming. Yet, enacting these identities meant that they did not study to catch up to their peers, ask their teachers for extra help, or ask their fathers to tutor them. Their identities did not require it.

College

College is often considered a site where youth prepare for professional jobs. Stay-at-home mothers had no intention of becoming professional workers, and so some saw college as unnecessary. This was particularly true for women whose mothers did not attend college; their own mothers provided proof that they could become stay-at-home mothers without a four-year degree. Virginia explained that she did not see the point of college. Rhetorically, she asked: "Why would I waste four years when I already know what I wanna do? I know where I wanna be, and I just felt that four years is too long."

Sarah tried college but found it was set up for people who wanted careers, not people who did not. Without wanting to become a professional and without the cultural resources to navigate it, Sarah felt at sea. She explained: "I went to college for a year and it was a waste. I wasn't really serious about it. I didn't really know how to do college. I didn't know what I was doing." Sarah did not report talking to her father about how to navigate college or seeking the help of the staff at her new school. Instead, she saw little reason to stay in college. She could become a stay-at-home mother without obtaining a four-year degree.

Rebecca did attend college. Both of her parents had attended, and she grew up assuming she would attend too. Moreover, with a college-educated mother who monitored her academics, she was more prepared to enter college than other women who identified as stay-at-home moms. She then attended college and navigated it in a way aligned with her identity. She majored in child psychology, not because she wanted a job in it—she did not know what jobs followed from her major, nor had she ever looked into it—but because she thought it would help her become a better mom. She did not care about her grades, either. Wanting to become a stay-at-home mother, she saw no consequences of a transcript filled with low grades, so she partied the night before tests. Rebecca also transferred colleges when she missed her boyfriend who attended a different university; doing so made sense as marriage was her priority. Expressing her identity left her no need to concentrate on her career options, grades, or academic skills. She concentrated instead on what was important to her—moving her relationship closer to marriage.[29]

Marriage

Marriage is central to the stay-at-home mother identity, and mothers with this identity worked hard to marry at a young age. Marriage itself does not require many resources to achieve, but, as we will see later, marrying without resources makes it difficult to stay in the upper-middle class.

Virginia worked hard to marry young. At age 19, Virginia maintained: "I would love to be married by the time I'm twenty-three so that I could just be married for a while, 'cause if I'm gonna have kids, I wanna have my first one when I'm twenty-five." To meet her goal, Virginia became what she called "a psycho dating person," who felt like, "I have to have a boyfriend, otherwise what am I doing?" After her year-long high school relationship ended with her boyfriend cheating, she dated six more men over the next five years. Many of her relationships were far from satisfactory. In addition to dating a guy she wished she could make herself fall in love with, she also dated one person who she thought would respond to a woman telling him they are pregnant by asking, "How do I know it's mine?" Another man slammed her into her car so hard that her father threatened to call the police. Yet, Virginia was clear that she wanted to become a stay-at-home mother, so her unsatisfactory relationships did not deter her from working toward becoming a young wife. Rather, with each new boyfriend, she would think: "I'm gonna be with this guy for a while, this is someone who I can see a future with." At age 24, Virginia's thoughts became a reality. She reconnected with a childhood friend and excitedly agreed to marry him.

Similarly, Sarah and Rebecca tried to marry young. In her early 20s, Sarah called marrying her personal mission.[30] She dated several men until she found one she thought would marry her—at which point she met her goal to marry young. Rebecca met the person she would marry when she was 15 years old. She worked to maintain the relationship by visiting often when they were at different colleges then later moving to be with him. She married at 23, soon after graduating from college. Knowing who they wanted to be— wives and then mothers—there was little reason to wait to become it.

Work

Women who identified as stay-at-home mothers rarely imagined they could marry and not work. Viewing work as a financial necessity, at least for a time, they went about it in a way that fit their identities. They de-prioritized work by casting jobs as less important than their relationships, viewing work as temporary, and putting their husbands' careers before their own. Doing so was aligned with the stay-at-home mother archetype, but, of course, not with acquiring the work-related knowledge they needed to stay in the upper-middle class on their own.

Virginia, for example, cast work as unimportant to her identity. She observed the centrality of work to her father and vowed to be different from him: "My dad is super driven, right? Like super, I mean, my dad makes a ton of money. He's like whatever super successful person, and I'm just not that way . . . I don't want to be married to my work. Ever. Whatever I do, I don't want it to rule my existence." She continued: "[My dad] has a lot of responsibility, and I wouldn't even want that. Who wants that? It's like people who want to be president. I don't even understand that, like, why?" Though she grew up with a clear career goal— become a beautician—she still wanted to make work revolve around her relationships. She explained that good jobs were ones that left time for family: "I don't want to use all of my energy on people who you don't even know and go home and have nothing left for the people who are actually important to you personally."[31]

Sarah and Rebecca also framed work as secondary to their relationships. Sarah decided to take a working-class job but considered it secondary to her primary job as a mother. She revealed: "I just wanna work one or two days a week. I mostly wanna just be home with my kids." After graduating from college, Rebecca worked as a nanny. The job was also part time; she thought that if she found a second part-time job, she would never see her husband. She also viewed her job as temporary. At age 26 she said: "I hope to be a mom and for that to be my primary job."

Identity Fulfillment

Virginia, Sarah, and Rebecca all entered their mid-20s having partly became the people they always wanted; they became wives and hoped they would soon become mothers. They were ecstatic about their achievements. At age 24, Virginia described: "I always knew that I wanted to get married. I always knew that that was something that I really wanted . . . It's nice to finally be in a place where I'm ready, I know it's with the right person, and this is a track that I want my life to go. So that's been really exciting." She planned to continue to devote her life to marriage and motherhood. Asked about her highest life priorities, Virginia talked of her upcoming marriage and the other roles it would bring: "I wanna be a good wife; I wanna be a good mom." Asked, similarly, what would make her happy at age 40, she again prioritized her relationship, saying: "A good marriage that I put a lot of time and effort into."

Sarah, too, was happy and relieved to have become a wife. She called her wedding the happiest moment in her adult life. She described how she hoped her life would unfold in the future: "Hopefully stay married, and have a family, be a mom, raise kids."

Rebecca also was thrilled to marry and looked forward to becoming a mother. At age 26 she felt that her relationships defined her. She stated: "I know who I am in my relationships with others. I'm a good friend, I'm a good daughter and a good sister and a good wife, and I try to be that in all areas of my life. I put a lot of attention into all the relationships that I have." When asked specifically about her highest priorities, she included her marriage: "To be somebody that people really value, either as a sister or as a wife, and so on." But although Virginia, Sarah, and Rebecca all started to fulfill their identities as wives and soon-to-be mothers, their long-term commitment to expressing their identities as stay-at-home mothers would cost some their class position.

The Stay-at-Home Mother Identity and
Downward Mobility

Virginia, Sarah, and Rebecca all expressed identities that were valued in their families and championed in their communities. Their identities also made the most of the resources they inherited; not given the human and cultural capital to excel in school, college, and professional work, they formed identities that made a virtue of not needing them. Being a mother was the most important thing they could do, they thought. What did grades and work matter in comparison?

Not valuing what was not given to them—the academic abilities and cultural know-how to succeed in school and professional work—they did not seek them out. They focused on relationships over learning and becoming wives more than workers. Doing so had a meaningful consequence: they never saw themselves as college-educated professionals and never prepared for that life, ruling out one option for class reproduction.

They had another option for class reproduction—to marry a college-educated professional. But here their resource weaknesses haunted them too. Virginia, Sarah, and Rebecca looked to marry in the 2000s and 2010s—decades after women had surpassed men in obtaining college degrees,[32] after the monetary returns to a college degree rose for women and men,[33] and after the ability to feel financially secure came to rely on two earners.[34] In this era of new opportunities for women and more fleeting opportunities for economic security for all, professional men not only had more opportunities to meet professional women but increasingly sought them out as well. The majority of professional men now said they would rather marry a college-educated woman than a woman without a college degree,[35] and they acted on these preferences: most college-educated men who married in the 2000s married college-educated women.[36]

This new marriage market made class reproduction through marriage difficult for women like Virginia and Sarah. Without inheriting high levels of human and cultural capital and without an identity dependent on acquiring it, they did not attend college—or at least not for long. They then did not meet many college-educated men and did not develop the educational profile most college-educated men wanted in a wife.

Removed from the marriage market that could offer them class reproduction, Virginia and Sarah married men who moved them further toward downward mobility. Virginia agreed to marry a soldier who had enlisted in the military upon graduating from high school. Sarah married a military man too. These men worked in jobs that depended on having stay-at-home wives—their forced and possibly frequent moves made a spouse who did not work for pay a good match for a soldier. Yet, while Virginia's and Sarah's marriages would allow them to be who they wanted to become—married stay-at-home moms—they did not keep them in their class. Their own identities ruled out class reproduction through becoming a college-educated professional, and their husbands' educations and jobs ruled out class reproduction through marriage.

Rebecca inherited more resources than Virginia and Sarah. Her stay-at-home mother had graduated from college, and Rebecca said her mother encouraged her to attend college too. Rebecca, who was raised with a particularly high amount of economic resources, was also taught to keep them—to marry a nice guy with money. Rebecca's greater human and cultural resources positioned her to attend college and marry a college-educated professional; her mother's suggestion that she marry a nice rich man encouraged her to seek a professional to marry too. She did. A year after her long-term boyfriend began medical school, they married.

Thus, for each woman, the path toward or away from downward mobility was shaped by their husbands but began long before they met them. In general, women like Virginia and Sarah—women without college-educated mothers—inherited fewer resources, did not complete college, and met and married working-class men. It was only women like Rebecca—those whose mothers had college degrees and offered them more academic and institutional resources—whose marital vows did not include a commitment to beginning their adult lives outside the upper-middle class.

The Surprise of Downward Mobility

Some women anticipated their own downward mobility, and others did not. After she decided not to attend a four-year college, Virginia's father warned her about her impending downward mobility. He urged her to change course—to attend college, marry someone who could better support her, or at least figure out a 10-year economic plan. Virginia appreciated his concern but ignored it. She was prepared to give up her six-bedroom house and to never again be part of a family that owned three cars. She wanted identity maintenance, not class maintenance, and she was excited that she found it.

Sarah was not so sanguine. In fact, she was surprised and outraged by the turn her life had taken. She imagined becoming someone like her mother and marrying someone like her father. She was shocked that she had not. Her husband left the military soon after they married and cycled between low-wage jobs and unemployment. She tried to talk him into finding steady work, but over four years, he never did. Sarah never imagined this fate—a life without economic security and a marriage to a man who was not a provider.

Why did Sarah not foresee her downward mobility? She always imagined having a life like her mother's but had not understood that *generational change* made it unlikely. Her mother married in a different period—in a time when it was more common for professional men to wed women who did not finish college or work in professional jobs.[37] In fact, around the time when Sarah's mother married, less than half of women ages 25 to 44 held full-time jobs, to say nothing of full-time *professional* jobs.[38] Most heterosexual men then had no choice but to marry a nonprofessional spouse. But Sarah's mother's marriage market was not the same as her own. By the time Sarah searched for a spouse, college-educated men were more likely to seek out college-educated women.[39] Sarah did not realize this or the implications of it: if she replicated her mother's resources and identity she was likely to enter a different social class. Furthermore, she did not realize that the labor market had changed for men without college degrees—finding steady and high-paying work had gotten harder.[40] If she wanted to stay in her class or experience economic stability, she needed to do what her mother had not done, what her family had not prepared her for, and what her identity did not make her think was necessary—she needed to earn a college degree.

Moving Forward

We leave Virginia, Sarah, and Rebecca when they were in their mid-20s. Their futures were unwritten, but they were likely to unfold in predictable ways. Women like Virginia and Sarah would likely stay on downwardly mobile tracks. They identified as stay-at-home mothers for over a decade, and now, so close to fully enacting each part of their identity, they were unlikely to switch course. Moreover, even if they did loosen their identity and pursue a college degree, it would be an uphill battle to complete them. With kids on the way, they would have little time to study. Their husbands would not be able to easily complete college either; with a stay-at-home wife, they needed

to work to support the family. For women on downwardly mobile trajectories, divorce was unlikely to change their class position either. Divorce was a
mark of failure for women whose identities were so intimately tied to marriage, and even if they did divorce, they would re-enter the marriage market
for people without college degrees. Most likely, then, they would stay in the
class position they entered as young adults—a class position that was below
the one in which they started. For women on class reproduction trajectories,
their futures were less predictable. They would remain in their social class
if they remained married but fall from it if they divorced or their husbands'
careers unraveled.

Virginia's, Sarah's, and Rebecca's trajectories then unfolded in a systematic way. They grew up without resources that would help them stay in their
original social class and developed an identity that made acquiring them
seem unnecessary. Men in the next chapter experienced the same resource
weaknesses and grew up in the same communities, though they held different identities. Their identities as family men opened up more opportunities to avoid downward mobility, though some still started on that path.

4

Family Men

A companion to the stay-at-home mother, the image of the family man is a married father who works to support his family. He's the man who plays catch with his kids, cheers from the sidelines at their soccer games, is home for family dinners, and tucks his kids into bed. In terms of work, he's a steady and reliable worker but not an ambitious one. To the extent that he can and still provide for a family, he distances his time and emotional energy from work. He may even look down upon career achievements as a sign of misplaced priorities—of not showing enough dedication to family.

The idea of the family man has been around for decades, and in the 1950s it enjoyed prominence. Marriage was obligatory at this time—nearly everyone did it—and all men were expected to work.[1] The family man ideal brought together these two spheres and suggested that men find meaning in their intersection—as providers and married fathers.[2] Television shows like *Leave It to Beaver* advertised the image of the family man, setting it as an ideal that men were expected to desire.[3]

As time went on, the family man model continued to be available to American men, but its contours changed. Ideas of a strong marriage evolved from strict gender roles in which men and women completed different tasks to ones of best friends working together to perform overlapping duties.[4] With a best friend at home, men were now expected to return home after work rather than heading to the bar to be with their real friends—other men.[5] Ideas of a good father changed too. Though still rarely in charge of parenting, men took on more responsibility for their children and were expected to receive more joy from raising them.[6] Moreover, given that men's involvement in family life was still not taken for granted, the men who spent substantial time with their families were showered with praise.[7] Being a family man could be a high-status identity.

Many upper-middle-class men grew up observing family men or hearing of them. The idea was encouraged in rural areas and the heartland of the country. Compared to firms in urban centers, white-collar firms in more rural areas were less hierarchical and fielded fewer applications from regional outsiders.[8]

Privilege Lost. Jessi Streib, Oxford University Press (2020) © Oxford University Press.
DOI: 10.1093/oso/9780190854041.001.0001

With less competition for jobs and fewer opportunities for promotion, there was less reason for college-educated men to throw themselves into school and work and more time available for family. Moreover, upper-middle-class boys in blue-collar towns could observe working-class men enact the family man identity. Manufacturing jobs advertised that they paid a "family wage"—one that allowed men to relieve their wives of working while still providing for their children.[9] Rural schools and families also prepared their sons for the jobs around them rather than the more competitive jobs in cities. They did so by emphasizing aspects of the family man image—emotional and time distance from school and work and greater connection to community.[10]

Conservative religions, too, pushed the model of the family man. They had long propagated the idea of strict gender spheres, with the man as the provider and the woman as the homemaker. Yet, as the economy changed and it became more difficult for their congregants to perform these roles, they offered a new image of an ideal husband. Instead of only being a provider, men were now also expected to be valued for the time they spent at home. Conservative Christian churches even went as far to suggest that careerism was undesirable; men should work but prioritize family over career.[11] The Protestant Reformed Churches of America put it this way:[12]

> Few husbands however know that this is required of them by the Lord. Most of them refuse even to sacrifice small things such as their own pursuits and pleasures in life. They give themselves wholly to their careers, and their family soon becomes very secondary. The time and energy that he should be giving for his wife and family is instead given to other things. He imagines that he is justified in that he is providing well materially for his family. But in our age of materialism and advancement in one's profession many husbands neglect the real needs of their wife and family and are in actuality seeking their own glory and wealth in the world. Very often husbands would do far better to spend a little more time with their families.

The Protestant Reformed Churches of America continued: "How little time fathers in many homes spend with their children. This is very serious and will contribute to the decline of the Christian home. Being too busy at work is a very poor excuse." James Dobson, among the most prominent evangelical Christian leaders, advocated that men prioritize family over careerism as well: "Sadly, many young fathers today see their children's mother as the primary caregiver and nurturer in the family. But kids clearly need their fathers just as much, in some cases even more. Fathers, take time for your children. Don't let your career absorb all your time and energy."[13]

Mormon churches also encouraged their members to become family men. Though the church emphasized education and finding "honorable" occupations, it also positioned work as a way to provide and family as men's top priority.[14] The Church of Jesus Christ of Latter-Day Saints' *Eternal Marriage Student Manual* put forth: "The Lord organized the whole program in the beginning with a father who procreates, provides, and loves and directs."[15] Though men "have a sacred responsibility to provide for the material needs of your family,"[16] they also should not focus too much on career and too little on family. The manual instructed men: "The family is the most important unit in time and in eternity and, as such, transcends every other interest in life,"[17] and "the greatest work you will ever do will be within the walls of your own home."[18] In these conservative religions, families were valorized while careers were downplayed as a means to an end.

Culturally and religious conservative communities then pulled some men toward the family man identity. The role was given great importance—acting as a family man was critical to men's well-being, their family's well-being, and the well-being of their religion.[19] Of course, some men were pushed toward it too. Some conservative Christian families encouraged their children to focus on becoming devoted family members and religious adherents more than on school and work; they passed down few of the resources needed to succeed in the latter.[20] Some secular families passed down few resources too—though often for different reasons. Some did not see the need to pass down so many resources, and others could not due to their own marital issues, workplace commitments, health problems, or their children's ability to receive them. Both men of conservative religions and secular men who inherited relatively low levels of human and cultural capital often adopted the family man identity. It was not hard to see why. The family man identity allowed them to reject the institutions that would not celebrate them—school, college, and professional work—and to claim that moral fortitude and personal success came from the institutions in which they could achieve more: marriage and family.

Reproducing Their Identities and Their Resources

Men could find status from the family man identity, and many men enacted this identity as they moved through school, college, marriage, and work. Yet, enacting this high-status identity gave men raised with resource weaknesses reason to ignore them, not overcome them. Doing so was at odds with class reproduction.

School

High levels of success in school require academic skills and institutional know-how. Simon, a blonde and shy Mormon, inherited few of these resources from his parents. His parents both had bachelor's degrees and worked as professionals. However, they did not transfer their resources to him. Simon described his father as an elitist who belittled him more than helped him—even calling Simon useless and a jerk. Simon then avoided his father because he thought his father hated him. Simon was closer to his mother but described her as hands-off. She was stretched thin by working and raising Simon and his many siblings, and she did not always have time for Simon. When he asked her to homeschool him for his final years of school, she agreed but did not follow through. Simon described the situation: "It wasn't really homeschool. It was just me not going to school."

Raised in a conservative community by parents who gave him little academic or institutional knowledge, Simon adopted an identity that made a virtue of his resource weaknesses and that was celebrated by those around him. He saw himself as a family man. In fact, at age 17, he had not considered his future outside of having a family. He had the following conversation with the interviewer:

INTERVIEWER: When you do think about the future, what do you think about?
SIMON: I think about having a family someday.
INTERVIEWER: What do you imagine you will do with your life when you are an adult other than having a family?
SIMON: I'm not really sure.

Seeing family as the main part of his future and his identity, he displayed the family man identity in school. The image of the family man is one of working but doing so with minimal time and emotional commitments. As a teenager, Simon could not yet be a full-time worker, but he could express this identity by putting minimal time and emotional commitment into his schoolwork. He said he received grades of "meets and exceeds expectations" from his high school and had a "laid back" attitude about his grades. After leaving public school, he signed up for a homeschooling correspondence course, but did not put too much time into schoolwork; he did not complete the program.[21]

Joe was a talkative young man with gelled black hair who grew up in a secular family in a heartland state. Like Simon, Joe described his parents as providing him with relatively low levels of academic and institutional knowledge. His parents both held master's degrees and each worked as professionals. Although Joe's parents had high levels of resources, they did not pass many onto Joe. Instead, Joe often hid from his parents, who regularly fought before separating when he was 15 years old. Joe lived with his father after the separation, but Joe confessed that his father acted more like a big brother than a dad. Joe described him as hands-off in regard to school and life decisions; they talked more about cars and relationships than school and work. And while Joe's mother tried to advise Joe about how to improve his grades, after years of hiding in the basement to avoid his parents' fighting, Joe was no longer amenable to her advice. Joe's father instructed Joe's mother to back off too—to let him find his own way. Even if he had not, Joe may have found his mother's academic advice difficult to use—Joe had a learning issue that made it difficult for him to internalize the academic and institutional lessons his mother imparted.[22]

Receiving and accepting limited academic resources from his parents, Joe gravitated toward the identity that made a virtue of his limited resources. He grew up seeing himself as a family man. When asked who he admired, he pointed to his parents and said it was because they enacted the characteristics of family men (despite that, as he downplayed, they lived apart): "Probably my parents. They get along. They're one of the few marriages that I've been around that lasts and they both hold down good jobs and they seem to be happy with where their life is at. I really have to admire someone who is able to do all of that and keep it in balance." Through the lens of the family man identity, Joe took this balanced approach to school. He received Bs in school. Instead of studying more or asking his mother how to turn his Bs into As, he decided that Bs would enable him to later find a job. It was better, he thought, to spend his time and emotional energy dating.

Terrence was a slender man with a constant smile who wore polo shirts and a blue earring. He was also a family man—but, unlike Simon and Joe, he was a family man who did not inherit resource weaknesses. His mother and father both had college degrees, and both transferred their resources to him. His stay-at-home mom homeschooled Terrence when he was young and carefully monitored his academic work. At age 15, Terrence described the situation: "My mom, she was very, very smart growing up. She always got good grades, so she makes sure I study hard." Terrence said his father did not pressure him as much about school but did prepare him for work. At age 15 he mentioned: "[My father] just bought a new business and he's teaching me how to do things with that business and what it takes to run a business. He's just preparing me for when I get older and start working." A few years later, Terrence said his father taught him more about business, recommended finance books, and let Terrence shadow him at work.

For Terrence, the family man identity was mostly appealing due to his faith and the model he observed in his own family. An evangelical Christian, he talked about family and religion in the same breadth. At age 15, asked about the most important things in life, he said: "God and our country and my family and then me. That's my order." As a teenager, he also observed the family man identity in his own father and wanted to replicate it. He said: "I look up to my dad the most . . . I look up to the way he's approached his marriage. He's great to my mom, and I want to be like that when I get married and get older. He's really good with money and making sure that we have plenty of food to eat."

With no resource weaknesses, Terrence could have strived for academic achievements. However, the family man identity is predicated on emotional and time distance from work, and Terrence followed this model in regard to school. He said that he was "not the best studier," did not focus on schoolwork as much as he could, and earned mostly Bs. He also said that he left his home-school group because it was too academically demanding. He wanted to attend public school where courses would be easier and he could meet more girls to date. Thus, unlike professional men like Bert (discussed in chapter 2) who threw themselves into academic work, family men like Simon, Joe, and Terrence distanced themselves from it.

College

Family men were apt to struggle in college. They entered college with little academic preparation and their identity compounded this issue. To express a family man identity, they needed to distance themselves from schoolwork, and, as they were getting older, to invest more in romantic relationships. This approach to college put men's class reproduction at risk; many struggled to graduate from college.

Simon received limited academic knowledge from his family and "school"—making it likely that college would be difficult for him no matter what identity he adopted. His identity as a family man only furthered his struggles. Aligned with the family man identity, he expressed disinterest in schoolwork. At age 17, Simon said: "I guess college would be okay, but I feel indifferent toward it." At age 18, he enrolled in college "just to kill time" before he went on a religious mission. He never returned to college. His parents stopped financially supporting him after he returned from his mission, but, more than that, Simon did not see the point of earning a degree. College degrees, he said, were nice to say you had, but not necessary for the life he wanted to lead. At age 27, Simon had not completed a college degree and did not think he would.

Joe also entered college then struggled to remain there. He said he had an "ambition problem" in regard to his classes. He often skipped them to sleep or play video games; he also dismissed his mother's repeated advice to focus more on schoolwork. Instead, he spent his time and energy on the activities aligned with the family man identity: romantic relationships. Hoping to meet someone in college whom he would marry, he invested deeply in this effort—so much so that, like for other family men, it put him in academic jeopardy. At age 22, he recounted: "In the past two–three years [my frustration with meeting someone] definitely has driven me to fall back in school, just 'cause of not wanting to leave to go to classes much because maybe the girl that's sexy is not gonna wanna give me her number. So I feel like, 'What's the point? Why go? 'Cause I want a girl so bad.'" At age 27, he recalled the same issue: "When I was single I would look to some of the girls in my class and fantasize about asking them out on a date. And then I wouldn't have the courage to do that, so then I'd leave the class depressed because I wasn't able to talk to the girl next to me." Joe's commitment to romantic relationships showed his dedication to the family man identity but also discouraged him from attending his classes. He did not invest in gaining academic knowledge, failed courses, and dropped out of college for years.

Terrence entered college with more resources. His experiences differed from Simon's and Joe's—having inherited more resources, he could enact the family man identity and still graduate from college. He did not talk of devoting himself to his schoolwork like Nancy, Molly, and Bert (discussed in chapter 2), but he did not need to in order to meet his goals. He majored in business, a field that rewarded him for the knowledge he already inherited from his father. Enacting the family man identity, he also spent his college years devoted to dating. With more academic and institutional knowledge, doing so was not too great of a distraction. He graduated from college in under four years.

Marriage

Marriage is at the core of the family man identity, and men with this identity wanted to marry young. Simon was eager to marry. Soon after he returned from his mission trip, he opened his front door to see a woman he barely knew. She said, "So, we gettin' married?" Despite his surprise at her proposal and that they had only briefly met, Simon immediately agreed to marry her. Marrying would allow him to become a family man.

Joe worked hard to marry young. He dated so seriously in high school that after a breakup, he referred to himself as a divorced dad. He continued to seek serious relationships for the next decade and dated a handful of women he hoped to marry. These relationships ended, but by age 27, he was in another serious relationship with a woman he planned to marry. Aligned with the family man identity, Joe saw his relationship as a major accomplishment. At age 27, he said: "I see that as my biggest achievement over the course of my life because once you find that one person that you're happy with, nothing else matters." He also described his relationship as fulfilling his identity: "I'd say the number one thing [that makes me happy] would be my girlfriend . . . Because I feel that my life is leading somewhere—that I'm going to accumulate that family life that I wanted and dreamed of as a child."

Terrence, too, made a point to marry young. At age 15, he hoped to marry around age 21. At age 16, he began a two-year relationship, and at age 18, he began dating the woman who would become his wife. By age 22, he was married. He called his relationship with his wife one of the most important parts of his life.

Work

In addition to marrying young, family men also wanted to become providers. For example, Simon took a working-class job after leaving college. He thought the job was boring but saw it as an important way to support his family: "I wanted to have a job, obviously. I had a wife and a kid." Joe also thought of work as a way to provide for a family. At age 22, as a single man, Joe framed his first commissioned internship through the lens of a family man: "I gotta do this then that, if I don't get it done, I'm not gonna be able to put food on my table and my wife's gonna suffer because of that." Terrence thought of work in a similar way. At age 15, he saw himself as a provider for a future stay-at-home wife: "I think it is a lot better when the mothers don't work, that they're more there for their kids." At age 23, he filled out paperwork as a benefits analyst. He found the job boring but planned to stick with it. He needed to be a provider.

Following the family man model, men also distanced themselves from work emotionally. They showed disinterest in the content of their careers and in career advancement. At age 17, Simon had no career goals. After leaving college, he fell into the working-class job that he found through a friend. At age 27, after working this job for several years, he had given little thought to what else he might do. Asked about his future career plans, he alluded to a childhood dream then laughed as he revealed he had not given much thought to the question: "Hopefully I'll be a writer. If not [laughs], then I guess I'll be [in my current job] for the rest of my life!"[23] Similarly, at age 17, Joe had given little thought to his career. Asked what he wanted to do for work, Joe said: "I don't really think about it too much." At age 22, he thought about work more, but in a way that showed his disinterest. He presented work as a future chore, not as a place to invest his emotional energy: "One of the biggest thoughts that runs through my mind is—it's a dark thought, a depressing thought, but my friends and I talk about this a lot—having to work a job that you don't necessarily want to work, and coming home to a house that's average, and waking up and doing the same thing over and over again." Terrence concurred that work did not hold his interest or preoccupy his plans. At age 23, he said: "I think a lot of people base their purpose on their career objectives. I am very purpose-driven, but as far as my career, I had no idea I was going to be doing benefits, and I don't know if I wanna do benefits for a long time. I don't really know where I wanna go."[24] With an identity predicated on emotional distance from work, the content and future of their work never seemed particularly important.

Identity Fulfillment and Hopes for Their Future

As young adults, Simon, Joe, and Terrence were thrilled to be family men and looked forward to remaining family men in the future. At age 27, Simon was happy with his life: "Growing up, my only real goal was to be a family man, and so I'm very happy 'cause I've achieved that." He looked forward to a life as a family man too. He said he wanted "the whole experience, just having kids and grandkids."

At age 27, Joe, too, saw himself as a family man. In fact, a year earlier, he called his father to tell him: "I'm a family man now." Joe thought he would maintain this identity in the future: "I would say my purpose in life is to try and make [my girlfriend] as happy as possible, try to provide for my family, in the hope that we'll have an offspring . . . So my goal, my purpose in life is to provide for them." When asked to describe what constitutes a good life at age 27, Joe talked again of being a family man: "To have provided for my family and created a family."

As Terrence became an adult, he also experienced identity fulfillment. At age 23, he wanted to dedicate himself to his wife and future kids: "I would say my biggest priority would be continuing to develop my relationship with Christ, just to follow him, and just strengthening that every day. And then strengthening my relationship with my wife would be next. And then from there, once I have kids, I wanna be the best dad possible. That's gonna be a huge priority. But right now, I'm just focusing on being a good husband." Terrence saw himself continuing to be a family man in the future, too. "To be truly happy [at age 40], I'll need to be continually growin' in my faith and to continue to develop deeper relationships with my wife and my kids and my family in general. As long as I am continuously growing and deepening those relationships, I think I'll be ecstatic when I'm forty." As young adults, Simon, Joe, and Terrence then continued to enact the identity they long held. Yet, for Simon and Joe—those raised with resource weaknesses—doing so did not help them avoid downward mobility.

The Family Man Identity and Downward Mobility

Being born into the upper-middle class provides no guarantee of staying there. As they enter adulthood, one in two upper-middle-class youth begin to drop out of their original social class. Who does so is not random—it is usually youth raised with resource weaknesses and whose identities encourage their maintenance.

Simon and Joe were among those who inherited resource weaknesses. They received relatively low levels of academic and institutional knowledge from their parents, making it difficult for them to excel in school or professional work. They then developed family man identities that encouraged them to distance themselves from these institutions. Simon could have turned to teachers or members of his church for academic help. Once Joe's mother and father stopped fighting, Joe could have asked his mother for help with school or tried harder to follow the advice she offered. Once in college, Joe could have regularly attended his classes. Simon and Joe did not take advantage of these resources. Instead, aligned with the family man archetype, they distanced their motivation and time from school and work.

With the combination of his inherited resources and identity, it was not surprising that Simon entered adulthood on a downwardly mobile trajectory. Disinterested in school and not invested in any particular type of work, Simon saw no reason to remain in college or strive for a professional job. At age 27, he held a working-class job and did not have a college degree. Aligned with the family man identity, his wife did not work for pay, leaving him as the sole provider for two adults and multiple kids.

Joe was also on a downwardly mobile trajectory. Inheriting relatively little human and cultural resources from his parents and with a learning disability that made their transfers difficult to internalize and use, he developed an identity that discouraged him from acquiring more resources. He was content to get by in school and work and instead to focus on marriage. Doing so had consequences. At age 27, he had not graduated from college or worked in a professional job. Instead, he took college courses while working at a car repair shop.[25] He was also in a relationship but unmarried; he had yet to obtain class reproduction through work or marriage.

Like many family men, Terrence inherited more resources but adopted the same identity. The family man identity was esteemed in evangelical circles and in his own family, and he became a family man himself. He took the same approach to school and work as Simon and Joe, but, doing so with more inherited resources, he did not fall from the upper-middle class. Instead, he hung on by a thread. He did entry-level work as a benefits analyst—a glorified way to say that he monitored the paperwork attached to clients' benefit plans. Moreover, his spouse worked in a professional job, but he hoped she would become a stay-at-home wife soon. With little investment in the labor force, it was unclear how long he would stay in the upper-middle class.

The Surprise of Downward Mobility

Simon, Joe, and Terrence had different reactions to their class trajectories. Simon was just happy to be a family man; it was his only long-term goal. Joe was also happy to become a family man but was upset that he had yet to become a college-educated professional. Terrence was satisfied with his current position but anxious about the future. Joe's and Terrence's worries were misaligned with their effort in regard to school and work. Why did Joe and Terrence have trouble making the connection between their identity and class trajectory?

One simple reason can be ruled out. It was not that Joe and Terrence did not understand that a college degree and professional job were necessary for life in the upper-middle class. Joe had a clear understanding of the need to earn a college degree to enter the professional workforce; that was one reason why he kept working toward a degree at age 27. Terrence grew up assuming he would be a college-educated professional and in the upper-middle class. His father was his role model, and he assumed he would be like his dad.

Rather, the misalignment between their worries and their approach likely resulted from the difficulty in recognizing *generational change*. In Joe's and Terrence's eyes, their fathers were both family man and in the upper-middle class. Yet, while Joe and Terrence had less or similar academic knowledge than their fathers, they lived in a time when they needed more. Since their fathers became family men, the human capital requirements for becoming a professional mounted. Upper-middle-class students increased the amount of time they spent on academic activities, and family men of Joe and Terrence's generation were left to compete with students with higher test scores and GPAs.[26] Under-employment also rose for men with college degrees and those with some college too,[27] and many men with little human capital for their education level were pushed out of professional jobs.[28] In addition, professionals' work hours increased as well. Professional men, especially, were pushed to work longer hours than their fathers—something Joe and Terrence did not want to do.[29] In short, the link between being a family man and a member of the upper-middle class became more tenuous for Joe and Terrence's generation than their fathers'. Not all youth recognized or prepared for this change.

Moving Forward

Family men looked forward to a lifetime of marriage, fatherhood, and serving as a provider. As their futures unfold, it seems likely that family men on downwardly mobile trajectories will remain outside the upper-middle class. At age 27, Simon had a stay-at-home wife and multiple kids and hoped to have several more children soon. Needing to support his family, he did not anticipate returning to college or think his wife would either. Men like Joe who were still enrolled in college could graduate, but they would likely find it difficult to land professional jobs. They would need to compete with their peers with professional identities—those who entered the professional workforce at younger ages and who expressed more dedication to work. Furthermore, their desire to be the primary provider made class reproduction through marriage unlikely. Though Joe hoped his future wife would work, many family men hoped their wives would stay home.

Men like Terrence—those raised with resource strengths and on class reproduction trajectories—were more common in the sample than family men raised with resource weaknesses and on downward mobility paths. However, they had no guarantee of remaining in the upper-middle class. The professional labor market increasingly rewards men who live to work, but men like Terrence were adamant that they work to live. This approach may leave them vulnerable to downward mobility; they would spend the rest of their lives competing for jobs with peers whose professional identities pushed them to work more. And, like family men on downwardly mobile trajectories, their hopes to be the primary provider would do little to encourage their wives to save their class position. Though Terrence was in the upper-middle-class today, he could be out of it tomorrow.

5

Rebels

Rebels fell down the class ladder. Their resources poised them for a fall, and their identities pushed them over the cliff.

Kyle was a casually dressed young man with curly brown hair with blonde highlights. He grew up in a liberal town. His parents had substantial economic resources—enough to send Kyle to boarding school and college. Kyle's father was a college-educated business owner but did not pass his academic skills and institutional knowledge to Kyle. They rarely interacted. Instead, they watched the same baseball game in different rooms, and, when they did see each other, they talked only of sports. Kyle's stay-at-home mother, who did not possess a college degree, was not prepared to pass down as many resources to Kyle. Of course, in Kyle's case, his mother's education hardly mattered as he rarely spoke to her too. As he put it: "I wouldn't mind talking with her more, it just doesn't happen."

Daniel also received limited academic and institutional knowledge from his parents. Daniel, a young man with brown hair and brown eyes, grew up in a liberal city as the son of a college-educated professional mother and a college-educated father who worked in a working-class position. His parents' earnings were fairly high, but Daniel also described his parents as hands-off. He explained: "They've always been very respectful of my right to be an individual, and they never really push too hard to get me to do anything. They've always trusted me to live my own life and make my own decisions." Though Daniel appreciated his parents' approach, it also meant that they only occasionally pushed him to develop academic or institutional knowledge.

Colin, a tall and pudgy man with blonde hair and blue eyes, grew up with the same resource profile: he inherited limited human and cultural capital from his parents. His parents divorced when he was a few years old. Colin then lived with his mother in a wealthy and liberal community and periodically visited his father, a computer engineer who Colin said earned a quarter-million dollars a year. Colin recalled times when his father "lost his temper, smashed up the house, stuff like that" as well as times when his father angrily yelled and swore at him. Colin thought his father's children from his first marriage were justified in

Privilege Lost. Jessi Streib, Oxford University Press (2020) © Oxford University Press.
DOI: 10.1093/oso/9780190854041.001.0001

not talking to his father given his pattern of disruptive behavior. Unsurprisingly, then, Colin never described his father as someone with whom he talked to about school, college, or professional work. Colin's mother, a graduate-school-educated manager of computer scientists, repeatedly tried to teach Colin about school, college, and professional work. Yet, whether it was because his parents were hands-off before they divorced, a learning disability, or a mental health issue, Colin did not accept his mother's resource transfers. He seemed to learn early on that he was behind in school and refused to catch up.[1]

For upper-middle-class men in liberal communities, growing up with relatively low levels of academic skills and institutional knowledge created a toxic mix. Having received or accepted little academic knowledge from their parents, these men were unlikely to be celebrated by schools, colleges, or professional workplaces. In communities that urged delayed marriage, they were unlikely to be applauded for marrying young. There was then no institution that would prop them up as pillars of the community or even give them status. They responded by opting out. They rebelled against each institution and the adults who pushed them into them. As young men, they could receive recognition by acting as rebels. They did so, losing their class position in the process.

Resources, Communities, and the Rebel Identity

The cultural image of the rebel is a young person who revels in their rejection of institutions' and parents' rules and expectations. Rebels strive to be beholden to no one but themselves, and they show their independence by openly defying authority figures' instructions. They want freedom to do what they want, and they work hard to show that no one—not a person nor an institution—controls their actions.

The archetype of the rebel is all around us. It is shown to children in cartoons like *Denice the Menace* and *Calvin and Hobbs* and portrayed to teens and adults in films like *Fight Club, The Breakfast Club, Rebel Without a Cause,* and *Ferris Bueller's Day Off.*[2] These fictional rebels are mostly boys and men portrayed in a high-status manner. They are cool and macho, independent and agentic. They are heroes to some and annoyances to others—but only to those who wish to conform to the norms of dull and backward institutions.

The image of the rebel is consistent with many of ideas of masculinity—men are independent, resistant to others' rules, and agentic[3]—and some parents encourage these traits, although not always directly. Parents often tell boys to be tough, and therefore not reliant on others; in control, and therefore not subject to their environment; and powerful, and therefore agentic regardless of their situation.[4] Some girls are encouraged to adopt these traits too—though rarely to the extent as their brothers.[5]

Of course, most upper-middle-class youth do not become rebels, regardless of the images they see in the media and the agency their parents teach them at home. The rebel identity is mainly useful for those who need to solve a problem—to gain status despite having few resources that institutions reward. The rebel identity tells others that youth do not define their worth through institutions but against them. It frames their low levels of achievement in traditional domains as a choice rather than as a consequence of limited resources and abilities.

Kyle, Daniel, and Colin adopted this identity. Kyle described his teenage years: "When I was away for high school and then for college I peaced out and was being rebellious." At age 17, Daniel said he enjoyed playing the rebel. He stole, he said, "Just to be bad. Just to break the law or do something wrong." Daniel also regularly used drugs, which he attributed to his desire to fit a particular image: "I think popular culture displays teens as people who like to do drugs and try different things. You know, adventurous people." Daniel defended his rule breaking, too: "[My parents] want me to learn to follow the rules, but I think what I'm doing is okay."

Colin rebelled too. Much of his early rebellion was directed at his parents, especially his mother. He said of lying to his parents: "I think if you don't lie at all and you follow them in every wish, that's a problem." He called his parents "assholes" and looked forward to college as a time when "no one busts my balls." Meanwhile, he tried to get away with as much as he could—including parties and drug use. He drank alcohol and smoked marijuana on school property, and before he graduated from high school, he was arrested for drug use.

Kyle, Daniel, Colin, and others like them would continue to rebel as they grew older. Doing so would cement their identities as rebels—an identity that discouraged them from gaining the resources they needed to stay in the upper-middle class.

Reproducing Their Identities and their Resources

Rebels entered school, college, and work with few of the resources these institutions reward. Born into resource-rich communities and attending schools and colleges with stellar reputations, they could have acquired the resources they grew up without. Instead, they rebelled.

School

Rebels distanced themselves from academic work and broke institutional rules. Kyle adopted the rebel identity as he attended boarding school. At age 18, Kyle advertised his apathy toward academics: "I didn't really care as long as I was doing alright. I don't really care about the difference between an eighty and a one-hundred." Kyle also explicitly rejected his teachers' push to raise his grades, showing, again, his apathy about academics as well as his rejection of authority figures' advice. He explained: "I think there's a lot of pressure to be successful and go out and get a good job and get a good education. There's a lot of pressure to not stay where you are in life. Everybody tries to push you forward . . . There's people that respond to the pressure and pick up their studies or work really hard, and then there's kids that rebel against it. These people want me to work harder so I'm gonna work less just to spite them." Kyle put himself in the second group—he rebelled against earning high grades. He would not be held hostage to others' expectations.

Kyle also showed his identity as a rebel by countering school rules. As he put it, "My school was very strict. You could say that there were two groups of people there, people who played the game . . . and people that didn't; they were my best friends." Kyle routinely skipped classes, snuck out of his boarding school dorm room past curfew, and instigated pranks. He did not think about what was right and wrong as much as what he could get away with. He resented his teachers for enforcing rules: "I don't know whether they're looking out for you or jealous or what, but there's a lot of people that seem to try to stop the fun."

Daniel showed his rebel identity by disregarding academic coursework and school rules. When he was a teenager, Daniel's father pushed Daniel to bring up his grades. Daniel did not outwardly refuse, but he did not study more. Instead, he focused on breaking rules. In eighth grade he started smoking weed, and in high school he and his friends stole from local stores. He saw little wrong with either.

Colin displayed his rebel identity in high school as well. His mother was far more hands-on than most of the parents of rebels, but Colin did not accept or follow her advice. He explained: "It's always, 'Have you done your homework?' I can't watch TV or play video games without her giving me a hard time." He continued: "If I'm watching TV or playing a [video] game, I'm gonna keep doing it. Sometimes my mother, she tries to make a big deal out of it . . . She thinks that if I'm doing it, I'm obviously not doing my school-work. It's kind of true 'cause I don't really do much homework." Instead of doing homework, he spent time breaking rules by drinking underage and getting high.

Despite that Kyle attended a private boarding school and Colin attended what he thought was one of the best public schools in the country, neither of them, nor Daniel, took advantage of the resources their schools offered. Instead, they distanced themselves from schoolwork and school rules, doing enough to get into college but little more.

College

College offered rebels space to show their identity. For four more years, they could break rules and distance themselves from academic knowledge.

Kyle spent his college years acting like a rebel. He described his college ca-reer as marked by his time in a fraternity. He drank heavily nearly every night, even when he was underage. He saw this as the appropriate as his goals were to live for himself, not for a future job or wife. Daniel took the same approach. At a flagship state university, he spent much of his four years in college social-izing with his friends, getting high and drunk. To Daniel, this social scene fit his identity. Asked where he most belonged, he answered: "More than any-thing, with people who know how to have a good time."

Colin, too, spent his time in college rebelling. Early in his college career he was kicked out of college for drug use. After breaking more rules by faking community service—his punishment for getting high—he was readmitted into college. There he continued to rebel and disengage. He spent $30 a day to take a hit from his bong every fifteen minutes. Asked what made him happiest, he referred to breaking more rules: "Just having a good time . . . Just sit around and get fucked up, that's a good time."

In college, like in high school, rebels also displayed their identities by dis-tancing themselves from academics. Kyle's college GPA was low enough that he thought that all graduate schools would reject him. Daniel did not stress about his grades either; partying while studying abroad seemed much more important, as did spending time hanging out with friends. High most days,

Colin also received low grades in college, though he did not attribute them to his own actions. He explained: "In school, gay shit happens. I don't really have good enough grades." The rebel identity may have offered these men status given the resources they had, but their time in college did little to prepare them for professional work.

Work

Just as rebels opted out of schoolwork, they also opted out of professional work. Rebels saw professional work as opposing their identities by requiring rule following rather than rule breaking, conformity rather than independence, and a focus on others rather than themselves. At age 28, Kyle had never worked in a professional job, and had not applied to many. He did not like the idea of conforming, losing his independence, or focusing on others' demands: "I don't want to have people telling me what to do."

At age 27, Daniel also had applied for few professional jobs. He saw professional work as requiring conformity and disallowing rebellion: "It's like you lose your real personality. You have to adapt to a certain cookie-cutter lifestyle, personality, world outlook, because to be too individualistic would threaten your status as an adult or would threaten your professional well-being, your career." Daniel also considered attending graduate school but decided against it. Graduate school, he thought, also involved too much conformity: "It's stifling. I don't really agree with the idea that you get skills and then market yourself. That takes so long. I'm more interested in living my life now."

Colin opted out of professional jobs, too. After trying and failing to become a teacher, he decided not to try to obtain a professional job at all. Instead, he turned to legally gambling on sports games and illegally reselling tickets to professional sports games. The work suited him. He did not have to conform to anyone else's demands, and he could use his illegal work to display his identity as a rebel.

Marriage

Youth can reproduce their class position through professional work or through marriage to a professional. However, just as rebels rejected professional work, they also rejected marriage. Being a rebel is predicated on showing independence from institutions and from others; marriage involves entering a new institution and forming ties with others. Rebels then put off marriage and even committed relationships, seeing them as at odds with their identities.

At age 28, Kyle had never been in a relationship that lasted longer than three months. He thought he might want to be single forever, but if he was with someone, he wanted to find someone who would not change his current focus on independence. He described the type of person he would be willing to marry: "I think it'd be an issue if they wanted to be with just me all the time, I think that would be a little too much."

Daniel, too, rejected marriage as a desirable option. Throughout his life, he avoided romantic relationships. At age 17, he thought that a committed relationship would stifle his independence: "I don't think I would like to get married until I'm into my thirties. I wanna enjoy my life for a long time before I settle down." At age 22, Daniel felt the same way: "I want to enjoy my bachelorhood as much as possible, and there are some things that you can only do when you are a bachelor. I'm not talking sexual things, I don't want to have all these female conquests or anything, but I want to travel a lot and I want to be on my own and be free to do whatever comes my way." At age 27, Daniel was in an on-and-off relationship. Asked about committing to her for a long period of time, Daniel waffled. He still saw relationships as opposed to his independence: "That scares me, the idea of just being with one person, the same person for the rest of my life. So I would say no to that although I'm conflicted. The idea of being with the same person for the rest of my life terrifies me on a certain level just because it rules out some other possibilities."

Colin also avoided romantic commitments as they countered his identity as rebel. He framed relationships as tying him to others' expectations rather than propping up his independence. At age 17, Colin talked of maintaining his independence rather than dating: "To girls, I'm not gonna become their bitch. I have my standards, I have my way of living, I have my things I have to do." At age 20, Colin also avoided committed romantic relationships for the same reason: "[These women] were fucking crazy. They were just trying to chill every day and shit. They were just trying to make me their boyfriend, and I wasn't down." At age 22, Colin still avoided relationships: "I'm not gonna be wasting a significant portion of my life doing what some girl wants me to do. 'Cause even just going out and getting shitty with your friends, your girlfriend doesn't like that and it's like, 'Man, that's what I like!' I like hanging with my boys and when sports are on I like betting on them and screaming at the TV when they're losing: 'Oh, you fucking asshole!' Girls don't really like that." Colin also thought that the institution of marriage could stifle his independence, so, if he married, he planned to rebel against its prescriptions about monogamy: "If your wife gets fat or she doesn't let you have sex and you've got money to spare, nothing wrong with ordering a high class hooker."

The Rebel Identity and Downward Mobility

Kyle, Daniel, and Colin began their lives with great privileges but did not hold onto them for long. Their parents had high salaries, they lived in well-off neighborhoods, and they attended renowned schools. Yet, they grew up missing key resources. Compared with others born into the upper-middle class, they received or accepted relatively little academic and institutional knowledge.

Kyle, Daniel, and Colin could have acquired academic and institutional knowledge from many sources outside their families. Their teachers, peers, peers' parents, guidance counselors, and coaches could have helped them learn more. As they grew older, their parents tried to step in as well—encouraging them to raise their grades then to apply for jobs. Instead, they built identities that made a virtue of their early resource weaknesses. To them, the right thing to do was not to acquire these resources but to show how little they cared about them.

In rebels' case, receiving or accepting little academic and institutional knowledge and then displaying an identity that celebrated not having it was a recipe for downward mobility. By their late 20s, Kyle, Daniel, and Colin were all headed out of the upper-middle class. At age 28, Kyle had never worked in a professional job. Instead, his mother found him a part-time job as a driver. At age 27, Daniel had never worked in a professional job either. Since graduating from college, he served food at a casual restaurant—a job he hated. At age 28, Colin, too, had never worked in a professional job. He still gambled and resold sports tickets. His "jobs" did not pay enough to live on, forcing him to reside in his mother's basement. Having avoided acquiring resources that could keep them in the upper-middle class, each man graduated from college and then entered a downwardly mobile trajectory.

The Surprise of Downward Mobility

To outsiders, it may seem obvious that disdaining academic and institutional knowledge would lead toward downward mobility. However, Kyle, Daniel, and Colin did not experience their trajectory as obvious. Though they never had any occupational goals and some even questioned whether there was enough room for all upper-middle-class youth to stay in their class, they were still somewhat surprised that they were the ones living with their parents or struggling to pay their bills.

Their surprise may have been structurally produced. Kyle, Daniel, and Colin experienced *life course change*. For the first stages of their life course, their inherited resource weaknesses and identities did not limit their ability to move toward class reproduction. It was only after years of moving toward class reproduction that their resources and identities would become a liability—pushing them out of the class that had once tolerated them.

The first institutions that rebels were in allowed them to move toward class reproduction. Upper-middle-class schools fail few students and kick few out; Kyle, Daniel, and Colin graduated from high school with weak academic records and a long history of rule breaking. Colleges also admit and graduate rebels. Indeed, the early informal mission of elite colleges was to serve as a place where upper-class men socialized, focused on fun, and skated by academically with "gentleman's Cs."[6] When colleges started to raise their academic standards, they still provided spaces to rebel against academics and rules: they allowed fraternities to exist on campus or nearby, knowing that they were places where men cultivated their identities as people who resisted rules.[7] These fraternities continue to exist today, though places to display rebel identities are no longer confined to Greek houses, if they ever were. Many colleges organize and sponsor parties and alcohol-filled sporting events that serve as places where students show their distance from academics and rules.[8] At some colleges, the anti-academic side of the university is so dominant that lawyers inform colleges that they cannot legally advertise themselves as offering quality educations—to do so would be to misrepresent the truth.[9] Many students engage in this side of the college experience; on average, students spend more time socializing than studying, and researchers estimate that there are more students whose priority is partying than there are students whose priority is academics.[10]

Colleges then provide a space for youth to cultivate and display their rebel identity, all while staying in an institution known as a gateway to the upper-middle class. Kyle took advantage of this at a private liberal arts college, Daniel at a flagship public university, and Colin at a reputable private university that he was surprised admitted him. They spent their time at college partying, but, as colleges allow, they still graduated about on time.

It was not until they left college that they were hit by life course change. Their identities had been tolerated and even encouraged by the first institutions that moved them toward class reproduction—school and college—but they would not be tolerated or encouraged in professional jobs. Professional employers expect a degree of conformity to their mission, rules, and routines; they have no reason to hire employees who are more interested in breaking rules than following them. Rebels knew this and did not apply. Still, for most of their lives, their identities were compatible with class reproduction. It was only in their 20s that they suddenly were not.

Moving Forward

Despite being dismayed about their downward mobility trajectory, rebels left the transition to adulthood with little idea of how to change it. They had no concrete plans about how to move forward and few accurate ideas about the labor force.

At age 28, Kyle had no idea how to move forward. He explained: "If I could pick an industry or a place, even a location that I wanted to be, I think that would help narrow things down, just make it easier instead of looking all over the place. Looking for work in four big cities and doing whatever is broad, and it's just tiring to shoot for a target that you don't know where it is." At age 27, Daniel had not identified any career goals either. He revealed: "I don't want to serve food for the rest of my life, but I still don't have a clear idea what it is I want to do."[11] Colin gave up on trying to find a professional career. If he accidentally had a child, he figured he'd find a job stocking shelves at Walmart overnight.

Rebels were also unlikely to find professional work as they had false ideas about obtaining it. They tended to believe that jobs and opportunities should come to them, rather than that they would need to look for work. At age 27, Daniel planned to wait for someone else to offer him a life-changing job: "I'm still hoping that I have my day with destiny. I know that sounds too grand, but I'm hoping that something just falls in my lap and completely changes the current trajectory of my life." At age 22, Colin thought that opportunities are given not taken, and he was resentful that more had not been given to him. He revealed his logic: "Giving all that aid to Africa, all those billions, you're never gonna see a penny back. To me it's like flushing money down the toilet, 'cause people there overbreed, they can't feed themselves, and you're just encouraging a bad situation to continue. So, Bill Gates, Angelina Jolie, and Brad Pitt, if they gave their millions away to budding twenty-two, twenty-three year-olds like myself, or just people in similar economic standings, we'd actually do something with it." At age 28, Colin still thought that people succeed by waiting for opportunities to be given. He was upset that others had denied him the opportunities he believed he was owed: "Unfortunately I'm somebody who's from a rich [city] suburb, but my parents won't give me money for a business." He continued: "I don't have anybody that I could borrow twenty thousand bucks from to do my tickets. It's like 'Oh man, come on.' " Waiting for opportunities to come, these men would also wait to find stable jobs. Given their work histories, they might be waiting a long time, prolonging their downward mobility.

In sum, these men formed identities that solidified their early resource disadvantages and kept them on a downwardly mobile track. As the next chapter will show, it was not only early disadvantages in regard to academic and institutional knowledge that set up youth to fall from the upper-middle class. Disadvantages regarding money played a similar role.

6

Artists and Athletes

Max was a short brown-haired young man with a strong sense of purpose. At age 16, he held a specific goal: "I'd like to work as either a master electrician or a lay designer." Amber, a young woman with long brown hair, freckles, and a nose ring, had a clear idea of where her life was headed too. At age 18, she asserted: "I wanna be a photo-journalist." Cory, a tall, thin youth with an athletic build and who wore basketball shoes to two of his interviews, also knew what he wanted to do. At age 14, he maintained: "I love basketball. My dream is to become an NBA player when I grow up. I know the chances of that are slim. If I don't become a player, I want to work as a sports analyst or whatever. 'Cause I'm a big sports fan. That's really important to me. God is number one and sports are number two."

Max, Amber, and Cory all wanted to become artists or athletes—broadly conceived as people who define themselves through arts or sports, whether or not they participate directly. Most artists and athletes were on downwardly mobile trajectories, breezing through college before failing to find a stable or professional job.

Resources, Communities, and the Artist and Athlete Identities

The archetype of artists and athletes is of people who throw themselves into the arts or sports while claiming that these activities define who they are. They relate to the world through their medium, seeing the world through the lens of a camera, how it would appear on a canvas, or through sports metaphors. They dedicate as much time as they can to their craft. To them, all other pursuits are secondary.

The archetype of the artist is also one of living in "the economic world reversed"—one in which earning money is disdained.[1] The "real" artist makes art for art's sake. Legitimate and high-status artists are "starving" artists— those who are more dedicated to making art than money. Illegitimate and

Privilege Lost. Jessi Streib, Oxford University Press (2020) © Oxford University Press.
DOI: 10.1093/oso/9780190854041.001.0001

low-status artists are those whose work is mass-produced, sold to the general public, and profitable. These artists' motives are questioned as they may produce art for the "wrong" reasons.[2] Athletes are evaluated with a similar logic, though to a lesser degree. Athletes, like artists, are pressured to present themselves as economically disinterested. The authentic athlete loves the game. The inauthentic athlete uses the game to make money.[3]

Artist and athlete identities are appealing to groups who have particular resource profiles: youth who inherit more human and cultural resources than economic ones.[4] Human and cultural capital—whether developed directly at home or through the environments parents place their children in[5]—help youth become viewed as talented artists or athletes. Despite the mythology that artists and athletes have "natural" talents, most instead receive repeated lessons about their craft and about how to navigate the art or sports world.[6] At least in this study, however, youth who adopt artist and athlete identities tend not to inherit high levels of economic capital.[7] These identities allow them to make a virtue of their resource weaknesses: real artists and athletes disdain the pursuit of money over the pursuit of passion. They have little money because they made the choice not to pursue it.

Max was one such youth who grew up with this resource profile. His mother worked as a college-educated childcare worker and his father as a scientist with a graduate degree. Max attributed his interest in technical theater to his elementary school music teacher—the person who first showed him how to prepare a stage for a concert or play. Having identified an interest, his mother facilitated it. They lived in a rural area and the nearest community theater was an hour away, so Max's mother drove him each way. By age 16, Max had spent over 400 hours at the theater. He worked directly under a master electrician—a mentor who taught him how to tear down sets, build props, and set lights. His investment in the arts corresponded to his parents' financial situation. They earned about half of Max's upper-middle-class peers' parents.

Amber was also raised with more human and cultural capital than economic capital. Her parents, both musicians with master's degrees, took her to museums and enrolled her in music lessons, ballet classes, gymnastics, and photography courses. They talked to her about her aspirations and how to meet them. They also modeled a lifestyle of living with little money for those with graduate degrees. Together, they earned about $65,000 a year and lived in an expensive and liberal coastal city. According to Amber, they lived in a rundown house and rarely traveled.

Cory, too, inherited more academic and institutional knowledge than money. His father, an engineer with a graduate degree, was laid off for years, and his mother, a school librarian with a graduate degree, did not earn much compared with Cory's peers' parents. Cory complained that he was the last one in his grade to receive a cell phone, the only one without a car, and that, unlike his peers, he had to work a part-time job. Still, Cory's mother provided him with academic and institutional knowledge. His mother worked at the conservative Christian high school Cory attended, and they regularly talked about what he was learning, how to navigate the school's politics, and how to apply to college.

In general, it was youth like Max, Amber, and Cory who identified as artists and athletes. Their academic and institutional knowledge allowed them to succeed in school and the arts, and their low levels of economic capital positioned them to find this identity appealing. Youth from both liberal and conservative backgrounds also gravitated toward these identities. Though many artists and athletes wanted to put work before marriage, nothing about the archetype ruled out the alternative order.[8]

Reproducing Their Identities and Their Resources

Max, Amber, and Cory expressed their identities as they moved through school, college, work, and marriage. Doing so had consequences. They could express their identity and move toward class reproduction while in school and college. However, upon graduating, their identity became at odds with class reproduction. Artist and athlete identities are predicated on the idea of prioritizing their passions while pushing thoughts about how to make money out of their minds—an approach that would lead to their fall from the upper-middle class.

School

Artists and athletes generally did well in school, though they displayed their identities by showing greater commitment to the arts or athletics. Max, for example, received nearly straight As and was the valedictorian of his high school class. Yet, Max's identity was never tied to school. He complained: "I've learned about Native Americans since sixth grade, every year. And I've actually had poetry shoved down my throat since then, every year. It just doesn't seem like it's a good thorough mix of things you should be learning." He complained, too, about homework: "I think teachers have a skewed vision. They somehow feel that homework should be piled on so that you can't have a life outside of school." Max thought that school and homework should include a bigger emphasis on an activity at the center of his identity: theater. He made this clear when asked about what excited him about college: "How much I could actually learn about what I want to as opposed to learning a lot of history or something . . . I want to learn about laying design and stage craft, building actual sets." Forced to be in a school that taught a traditional curriculum, Max spent as much time he could away from it. He spent weekends and vacation days at the community theater.

Amber also did well in school, but her passions laid outside it. She received mostly As, but, like Max, displayed more attachment to her artistic endeavors. During her high school years, she spent Saturdays at art classes and Sundays playing in a community orchestra. She also visited museums to admire the paintings and photographs, then became involved in photography herself. At age 16, she articulated her passion: "I love art. I like photography. I've gotten into photography a lot lately. It's nice taking your own pictures and developing them and seeing how you can make them better." She also expressed distaste for artistic pursuits that emphasized money. She avoided pop music because "in most cases it's about the money."

Cory's approach to school also highlighted his identity. Though he also received high grades, his focus was on sports. Cory claimed to be born athletic and saw school as a way to play soccer and basketball. Asked what made him most excited, at age 18, he answered: "Definitely the soccer team. I did not expect [to receive all-conference honorable mention] by a long shot, and sports is definitely a big thing in my life. There was [also] a basketball game . . . where I scored fifteen points in six minutes and that was the highlight of my basketball career." Cory thought that younger students looked up to him for his athletic talents, and he repeatedly expressed his love of the game.

College

Max, Amber, and Cory approached college in the same way that they approached high school—they did well academically but expressed their identities by throwing themselves into the arts or sports. Max chose a college with a technical theater program. After two years there, he moved to Europe. He enrolled in a European university but did so only for the visa. His main goal was to enter the non-unionized theaters in his new city so that he could launch his career. Once in Europe, he went straight to work, spending little time on his coursework and most of his time at the theater.

Amber also spent most of her time in college focused on her craft. She attended a university with a strong photography program and took most of her classes in photography. She displayed her photographs in multiple gallery openings—events she said were the highlight of her college career. She also spent her time interning as a photographer. Her friendships focused on photography too: "The friends I know from school, we relate to each other by doing photography." She used her time in college to express and reinforce her identity. Photography was the center of her life.

Cory also navigated college in a way aligned with his identity. He majored in sports management, interned for a professional team, found a job reporting one of his university team's scores, and became a freelance sportswriter. Though he gave up on becoming a professional athlete, he still identified as an athlete and remained tied to the sports world. For artists and athletes, college was a place to display and invest in their identities. Though doing so did not interfere with their ability to graduate from college, it would interfere with their ability to find professional jobs.

Work

Max, Amber, and Cory, like other artists and athletes, expected to find professional jobs after graduating from college. However, the image of the artist and athlete is one who follows their passions and shows disinterest in earning money. They followed this script, showing disinterest by not researching how to earn money in their field. Their disinterest in money made a virtue of their resource weakness but would do little to keep them in the upper-middle class.

The fact that they did not research how to earn money meant that they had little understanding of how difficult it would be to find professional jobs. Arts and sports jobs are in what scholars call a "winner-takes-all" labor market—one in which the best of the best earn sky-high salaries and enjoy job security while the remainder receive little at all.[9] Most jobs in arts and sports fields are project-based, low-wage, offer few benefits, and provide no job security.[10] Instead, cycles of employment and unemployment become a way of life, career tracks are difficult to find, pressure to work long hours is intense, and many entry-level jobs pay nothing at all.[11] Moreover, many who want to break into arts and sports industries never make it. Few people find jobs through formally advertised positions, and, instead, most hiring occurs through networks. If youth do not have the right networks, they are unlikely to be hired.[12]

Upper-middle-class youth are better positioned than most to break into the arts and sports industries. Their parents' economic resources may not be high for their class, but they are high enough to allow them to work entry-level jobs for low or no pay and to be free of financially supporting their parents. Their networks also tend to be more vast than aspiring artists and athletes from other classes, and their training in the arts and athletics more robust.[13] Still, most people, regardless of their original social class, do not find stable professional employment in the arts or in sports—there are not enough stable professional positions. Most upper-middle-class youth do not become exceptions. Youth with artist and athlete identities did not research the labor market—something that seemed crass to those whose identities were predicated on pursuing their passions—and were surprised when they struggled to find a steady professional job.

After graduating from college, Max hoped to pursue his dream of becoming a technical lighting specialist for a theater. He achieved this dream but found that work was allocated by show and that each job paid less than he expected. He hoped to find higher paying jobs and turned to designing and installing lighting for theater marquise, corporate events, and yacht owners. Struggling to make ends meet, at age 25, he surprised himself by leaving the theater world entirely. He took a job installing electronics in high-end homes.

Amber left college with the goal of becoming a photojournalist for a prominent newspaper—a goal that would be difficult to achieve in a winner-takes-all market. She did not find a job immediately after college and attributed her unemployment to the Great Recession. However, four years later, after the economy had improved, she had only found freelance jobs that offered low pay and no benefits. Still not understanding that she entered a labor market with few full-time jobs, she felt frustrated that her career had not unfolded as she planned. She maintained high expectations, taking it on faith that she would soon land a full-time position with the *New York Times*.

Cory also unknowingly tried to enter a winner-takes-all labor market. He gave up the idea of becoming a professional athlete as a teenager but expected to work in a professional sports team's front office. The idea came to him from watching *Seinfeld*, a fictional television show with a character who worked for the New York Yankees. Cory took the television show as evidence he could find a similar job and assumed his university would help him obtain it. At age 18, he said: "I like to think I know a lot about the NBA and certain sports I follow, but I don't know the managing aspects of it. But, hey, you need to learn some things in life and if it's a career so be it. I know that [the university I'm going to] has a good program for it so I'm excited to start learning what it takes." Yet, Cory never learned that the sports industry was a winner-takes-all field and that front-office jobs were few and far between. Instead, he graduated from college and expected to land a professional job in his field: "When I was in school, I thought once I graduate, I know the economy's tough right now but, hey, I'll have a college degree, I'll have a lot of experience. I expected once I graduate—maybe not right away, maybe not that summer I graduated but maybe in the fall—I would have a full time job." At age 24, Cory was frustrated that he had not found a job in a professional sports team's front office or a full-time job at all. Rather, he worked three part-time jobs: he ran a basketball league, played basketball with kids in an after-school program, and, in the summer, he organized a half-day sports camp.

In addition to feeling blindsided that they could not find steady jobs, Max, Amber, and Cory began to regret their earlier disinterest in money. They had substantial student loan debt—debt they had earlier taken out without concern for how they would repay it. When asked if he had any regrets in any aspect of his life, Max pointed to his earlier disinterest in money: "I wouldn't have gone to the university because it would have cost me less." Amber also expressed disinterest in thinking about money when she was a teenager—a choice she later regretted. When she chose a college, she said: "I'm going to have to pay back loans for a really long time. I would rather not pay that money but it's where I want to be. I don't like making [cost] the biggest factor." As a recent college graduate, Amber felt the same way: "It's expensive beyond belief. It was worth it to me." At age 26, she regretted her earlier disinterest in money: "I would have gone to a different school that was less money." Their earlier disinterest in money went along with their identities as artists and athletes but did not leave them with financial security or a professional job.

Marriage

Though they struggled to enter the upper-middle class on their own, artists and athletes still had the option of marrying into the upper-middle class. However, their identities were not tied to marriage, and most wanted to put off marriage until they had become the people they wanted to be. Marriage—and thus the possibility of class reproduction—would have to wait.

Max was one of the only artists and athletes who was married by the study's end, though he never intended to marry young. In high school he thought of dating as a distraction from theater and avoided it. He put off dating in college, too, until he met his wife. He fell in love with her, and, although he did not want to marry yet, he needed a visa to stay in her country. They married when he was 24 years old. As she was also an artist, their marriage did not interfere with his career—she followed him as he moved for his jobs. However, as an artist herself, she also did not change his class position.

Amber also imagined that she would marry after her career had taken off. In her life plan, she would find a prestigious and full-time photojournalist job immediately after graduating from college, marry at age 27 when her career was stable, and then have children a few years later. Her life did not follow her plan. Instead, as she approached age 27, she had neither a full-time job nor a full-time partner.

Cory, too, wanted to focus on his career before he focused on marriage. At age 18, he expected to marry after he finished preparing for his career: "You should be focused on your education and career first [before marrying]." At age 24, Cory, a committed evangelical Christian, still believed that he should find a professional job before marrying. Since he had not found a professional job, he had not yet dated. He explained: "I'm still single . . . I'm more of the person that I wanna get my career going first and then the rest will take care of itself." He reiterated that he was delaying marriage when asked if he did anything to find dates: "Nah, I'm boring. I'm just focused on getting my career situation situated." Seeing marriage as needing to happen after a career, not before, most artists and athletes entered their mid-20s untethered from each institution that could keep them in their class: marriage and professional work.

The Artist and Athlete Identities and Downward Mobility

Artists and athletes tended to inherit more human and cultural capital than economic capital. Their resource strengths corresponded to their ability to develop their artistic talents and succeed in school and college. But the artist and athlete identities also gave them a way to make a virtue of their resource weakness—money. It suggested that people like them prioritize passion over money and give little thought to how to pay their bills. This idea may have been comforting, but it did not offer them the focus they needed to stay in their class. Instead, they did not research the labor market and did not understand that they were entering fields with few professional jobs. As they left their mid-20s, Max worked in a working-class job as an electronics installer and Amber and Cory had not found steady work or professional jobs. Generally, artists and athletes were college educated but on downwardly mobile trajectories.

The Surprise of Downward Mobility

Max, Amber, and Cory were strong students who knew how to research the labor market and understand their job prospects. Yet, they did not put their skills to use, leaving them surprised that they entered adulthood without a stable professional job. Researching jobs—purposefully looking at ways to make money—was at odds with their identity. And, more than that, they did not realize that staying in the upper-middle class depended on it. Like rebels, they may have been misled by *life course change*.

Max, Amber, and Cory grew up in institutions that supported and encouraged their identities. Upper-middle-class schools often provide students space to pursue the arts and sports, and if schools do not provide these activities directly, upper-middle-class communities often do.[14] Upper-middle-class schools and communities also find ways to reward students who excel in these activities—giving them status through awards ceremonies, concert solos, and displaying their photographs on school grounds.[15]

Colleges do even more to reward upper-middle-class artists and athletes. Starting in the 1920s, elite universities began admitting students based on their artistic and athletic talents. These criteria initially provided colleges with mechanisms to discriminate against Jews, whose academic performance qualified them for admission.[16] However, after adding artistic and athletic talents to the admissions criteria, they took on a life of their own. Universities developed musical ensembles, theater groups, and intramural athletic teams to complement their academic services. As they needed students to fill these positions, they lowered their admissions criteria for artists and athletes.[17] Once admitted, colleges continue to support students' identities. Not only do they provide clubs for students to pursue their interests, but they also provide majors for students to cement their focus. Students transform from people interested in theater, photography, or sports to theater, photography, and sports majors.

Colleges are also touted as routes to the upper-middle class, and students may believe that their major will naturally lead to a job. Such a belief is not irrational. Investing in the arts and sports moved them closer to class reproduction for the entirety of their lives—first through being recognized in school and then through being recognized by colleges. However, once college ends, the life course bait and switch begins: artists and athletes are no longer rewarded by the institutions that support class reproduction. There are, simply, few professional jobs that could keep them in their class. Artists and athletes did not anticipate this change. It was sudden and defied the lessons that schools and colleges had taught them.

Moving Forward

As Max, Amber, and Cory looked to their futures, they did so through the lens of their identities. They maintained their goals, focused on pursuing their passions, and downplayed the need for money—despite that they regretted doing so in the past. At age 26, Max maintained that it was morally righteous to follow a passion: "I think that society as a whole doesn't allow people to really use their ability or whatever they have and tries to say, 'No, you're going to go into this box. You're gonna go and do this.' And so people basically are misguided and get sent off to go do, you know, a literature degree even though they'd rather be an electrician." He also still downplayed earning money: "Money isn't everything. It's important, but it's not everything. The work that you're producing should be the most important element to a job." Not focused on money, Max had little idea of how he would make it in the future. He just knew he wanted to keep working in a job that allowed him to be creative.

Amber's difficulties finding a job also did not lead her to reimagine her future. Instead, she continued to work toward the same goal, downplay money, and focus on following her passion. At age 26, she said: "I know I always want to be a photographer." She also continued not to worry about money: "I just think about how reputable who I'm working for is. I think that's more important than how much I'll be paid." She continued: "I would like to earn more, but I don't think that's as important as doing the work that I want to do."

At age 24, Cory had not found a professional job but still hoped to find a job in the front office of an NBA team. He considered going back to school to obtain an MBA, hoping that would make him more marketable. He gave himself some time until he did so, saying: "I'm hoping to work for a front of-fice in the NBA . . . I'm hoping I can just stay patient, believe in myself, which I have so far, ultimately some connection or some lucky break will get me a full time job in the sports world." Cory also downplayed the role money played in his future, playing up passion instead: "For my life to be a failure it would have been I had a good shot at doing something I love for a living and I gave up on it and I went ahead and did something for more money." He further justified his choice: "I've never been one for making the most money or doing something just for the money. Five out of seven days you'll be mis-erable and then you'll just be living for the weekend your whole life. So I've always been one for wanting to follow what I'm passionate about." Focused on pursuing his passion, Cory decided to keep pursuing a job in a winner-takes-all labor market.

Artists and athletes then wanted to remain on the path they embarked on long ago. As long as they continued to make a virtue of their early resource weaknesses—showing their disinterest in money and deep interest in their passion—they would remain in a winner-takes-all labor market and likely remain downwardly mobile. However, with college degrees, artistic talents, and sports knowledge, they had other opportunities open to them. If they could channel their interests into a professional job—even ones related to their interests such as graphic design, marketing for the arts or athletes, or becoming a teacher and coach—they may be able to turn their downwardly mobile trajectories into class reproduction ones.

7

Explorers

Communities and resources are not always aligned, and what resources individuals inherit are not always clear-cut. Youth in these situations tended to become explorers—those who held multiple identities at once.

Rhonda, a tall, fair-skinned red head, was one of several respondents who grew up in a particular contradictory space: she was a woman raised in a conservative community who was encouraged and given the resources to become a professional.[1] Rhonda's father worked two professional jobs; he was a teacher and a chief financial officer of a nonprofit organization. Rhonda realized that her father gave her the academic skills to become a professional. Her father regularly read the *New York Times*, debated politics, discussed novels, and talked about different cultures with Rhonda. He also brought her to his nonprofit and taught her to do his work. Rhonda's mother, who attended graduate school and worked as teacher, also helped Rhonda navigate school and learn about occupations. At a young age, Rhonda identified as a professional and chose a profession that her parents gave her the resources to obtain. At age 15 she exclaimed: "Probably I'll end up being a history professor!" At age 17 she said the same thing: "I don't know why I settled on college professor exactly, I've had that for years. I just found something the other day from when I was eight [years old] that says I want to teach history at Yale."

However, just as Rhonda's parents encouraged her to identify as a professional, they and their community encouraged her to adopt a different identity as well. Rhonda grew up in an evangelical Christian town, attended an evangelical Christian church, went to an evangelical Christian school, and lived in an evangelical Christian family. She observed the gender segregation at her school and the different expectations for men and women. She identified with the archetype that her religion pushed: women should be stay-at-home mothers. At age 17, Rhonda was committed to becoming a professor but also a stay-at-home mother. She claimed: "I think most girls are about not getting married, but I would be just as fulfilled if I was a stay-at-home mom as I would be if I was the President of the United States." She continued: "I

Privilege Lost. Jessi Streib, Oxford University Press (2020) © Oxford University Press.
DOI: 10.1093/oso/9780190854041.001.0001

think that women shouldn't be so worried about career if they're going to have kids." She held two goals at once—ones that reflected the identities available to her via her resources and community.

Reba, a short woman with short dirty-blonde hair and a shoulder tattoo, not only grew up in contradictory communities but also without a consistent set of resources. She described her college-educated mother, a former military member and then college-educated real estate manager, as both providing her with academic and institutional knowledge and as hands-off. At age 17, she said of her mother: "We have a good relationship because she's very educated, too, so we can sit down and talk about politics or just whatever comes up. She knows a lot more than I do, so she's a good person to learn from." However, Reba also described having limited interactions with her mother. At age 17, she said: "I don't see her very often, actually. I'm gone every day, I don't get home until about ten o'clock at night, so I see her for an hour in the evening and about an hour in the morning." She grew up feeling closer to her father, whom she described as informed and intelligent. However, her parents divorced when Reba was 8 years old, and her father moved to another state. Four years later, he died in a car accident. Reba was devastated. Of course, the academic and institutional knowledge she received from her father went away as well.

Reba also felt competing allegiances to conservative and liberal communities. She grew up in what she said was a conservative part of a southern state, one in which she observed women marrying young and becoming stay-at-home mothers. She also grew up spending summers and breaks with her father in a liberal northern state and learned that they did things differently. She internalized both views. She dated the same person from when she was 11 to 17 years old and imagined marrying him. At the same time, she said she could not understand why anyone would want to be in a relationship in high school or marry young. As she put it, "When you're just exclusive with one person in high school, it's just pretty foolish to me." And, despite having a long-term committed relationship in high school, she said that the liberal family model made more sense: "I don't think that sixteen and seventeen years olds have any business being in a relationship that is that emotionally draining. You're just not prepared. There's too many other things that you should be focusing on, like school instead of appeasing your partner."

Raised with inconsistent resources and exposed to environments that made contradictory demands, Reba internalized multiple identities. The human and cultural capital she received from her family allowed her to feel like a professional, and in high school she was determined to become a journalist in the military. Yet, she did not receive a consistent supply of academic and institutional knowledge from her family, and at times, as we'll see later, she felt like a rebel—opting out of organizations that might reject her and displaying an identity that allowed her to express anger about her father's death.[2] At other times she felt like a different person—she wanted to marry young and become the stay-at-home mom she thought her conservative community wanted her to be. She was an explorer—someone who held multiple identities at once.

Chris, a tall, lanky young man with long hair, sideburns, and hip glasses, inherited few resources for his social class. Chris's mother was a high-school-educated stay-at-home mom—someone he saw as a hippie and a caregiver but also as hands-off. Chris referred to his mother as unreliable: "She's a flake, but in the best way possible." His father held a master's degree and was employed as a professional social worker, but, as Chris put it: "He worked so much I hardly ever saw him." Chris believed that he learned little from his father: "I don't feel like I know him as well . . . My dad's always kind of been a mystery to me." His father's salary as a social worker was also low for the upper-middle class—he earned about $55,000 a year. Consistent with his low level of economic resources, Chris often imagined himself as an artist—as a future moviemaker. Consistent with growing up in a conservative state with low levels of academic and institutional knowledge, Chris also identified as a family man. He wanted to marry young and be involved with his kids, saying: "I've always been a Mr. Mom."

Rhonda, Reba, and Chris were explorers—youth who held multiple identities at once. Doing so reflected their early resources and communities and related to what resources they later tried to acquire. Women like Rhonda—those who identified both as professionals and stay-at-home mothers—worked to maintain the high levels of academic and institutional knowledge they inherited while also trying to marry young. With the resources they needed to become professionals or to meet and marry professionals, they often reproduced their class position—even if they felt internal turmoil along the way. Explorers like Reba were more often on downwardly mobile trajectories. To remain in the upper-middle class they needed to steadfastly maintain high levels of human and cultural capital—especially as they were raised with inconsistent amounts. They did so at times, but their other identities also led them to pursue other goals—leaving them vulnerable to downward mobility. Men like Chris often began on downwardly mobile tracks too. They hoped to combine being an artist and a family man, but the combination of the economic disinterest of artists and the flexibility of the idea of providing meant that they rarely acquired a full complement of resource strengths. Except for women raised in conservative communities by parents who gave them many resources, being an explorer often was aligned with inheriting resource weaknesses, maintaining them, and losing their original class position.

Reproducing Their Identities and Their Resources

The archetype of the explorer is now synonymous with emerging adulthood—it's the young person who tries on different experiences and selves. The explorer sees the value in multiple identities and feels drawn toward many. Depending on outsiders' perspectives, the explorer may be celebrated as well-rounded, adventurous, and open to many activities or derided as someone unable to commit to a single path.

Explorers like Rhonda, Reba, and Chris enacted this identity from adolescence through early adulthood, and they did so in regard to school, college, work, and marriage. Embracing this identity allowed them to feel true to the multiple parts of themselves. However, doing so meant following a nonlinear route to class reproduction or potentially not reproducing their class position at all.

School

Explorers used school as a site to express their multiple identities and to maintain the resources associated with each. As explorers held different combinations of identities, they approached school in different ways.

Rhonda expressed two identities while she was in school: a professional and a future stay-at-home mom. At age 15, Rhonda wore suits to school and described her life as "study, study, study." As part of her professional identity, she thought of herself as smart—so smart that she could not relate to her classmates: "I have a lot of trouble relating to normal teenagers just because if you're gifted and you're trying to make friends with somebody who all they care about is their hair ribbons [it's just not going to work]." At age 17, Rhonda felt the same way, calling herself "academic girl" and claiming an intellectual and future professional identity: "I'm an intellectual person where I really live in my head."

Just as Rhonda used school to express a budding identity as a professional, she also used it as a training ground to become a stay-at-home mother. Unlike Nancy and Molly, who saw their professional identities as at odds with dating, Rhonda, an explorer, thought she should commit to dating in high school too. She saw school as a romantic zone and recounted the school rules about who could date when, how teachers' courtships unfolded, and what happened at each dance. She felt lucky to be the only girl in one course with attractive boys but worried that she had not dated enough. At age 17, she complained: "We don't have a prom, but we have an equivalent. It's twice a year and for four years, and I have yet to get a date. Including Sadie Hawkins, so that's a little disappointing." She continued: "It's embarrassing to be the person that shows up to the party and there's three boys without a date and one girl without a date. And you're sort of going, 'There's a numbers problem here. How come I didn't get asked?'" To Rhonda, her lack of dating experience was distressing because she wanted six children and thought she needed to marry young: "I think that if you're thirty and you're not married, unless it's God's plan for you, you've probably missed the boat somewhere." Rhonda's expression of her professional and stay-at-home mother identities maintained her resources and frames—she collected more academic and institutional knowledge through her emphasis on school and stayed open to viewing school as a place to meet a husband.

Reba also used school to display multiple identities and maintain the resources she needed to enact them all. Reba yearned to become a journalist in the military. She kept her own grades high as she saw academic achievement and intelligence as part of her identity. She also looked down on others who she saw as failing in these ways: "With the rest of the school [who are not in AP courses], it's hard not to get a superiority complex, it's just hard not to no matter how hard you try." At the same time, Reba expressed her identity as a rebel while in high school. She broke rules by doing drugs, sneaking out of her house, and lying to her mother. Reba explained: "I've done every drug in the book except for shooting up; I'm scared of needles. I've done a lot of ice and a lot of coke and for about a year and a half, almost two years, I was smoking pot about three, four times a day. I was just continually stoned." Reba also expressed her identity as a stay-at-home mother. She spent much of her time in junior high and high school with her long-term boyfriend, who she talked of marrying. She maintained enough academic and institutional knowledge to express an identity as a professional and prepare for a future as a one, while also maintaining her identities as a rebel and stay-at-home mom.

Chris also expressed multiple identities in school—that of an artist and family man. At age 17, he articulated one of his identities: "I'm a socialite and I'm in drama." He called himself a "drama buff" who made videos for fun and who hoped to enter the movie industry. At the same time, Chris focused on romantic relationships—ones in which he showed that his commitment to acting as a loving and dependable partner outweighed his commitment to school. He dated continuously throughout junior high and high school, and all to women who he believed needed his help. In junior high he dated a girl whom he thought was depressed. In the first three years of high school he dated an anorexic woman. During his senior year, he dated a classmate whose brother was abusive and whose mother stole from her bank account. Despite the difficulty of these relationships, Chris stayed in them and sought them out. Doing so put him in a role his inherited resources prepared him for—that of a family man dedicated to romantic relationships. As these relationships took much of his time, they also took him away from acquiring the academic skills and institutional knowledge he would need to stay in his class. As he put it, "I had a 2.8 [GPA when dating one woman], so it's held me back academically."

College

Explorers attended college and displayed their multiple identities there. Of course, which identities they displayed related to which resources they acquired—and therefore the likelihood that they would or would not stay in the upper-middle class.

In college Rhonda continued to display her identities as a professional and a stay-at-home mother. Like professionals, she used college as a route to professional work. Still wanting to become a professor, she kept her grades high, worked as a research assistant, organized a conference session, and wrote a senior thesis. She also still considered herself smarter than her classmates, telling stories of shock that her classmates did not know that there were rivers in California, what the word manifestation meant, and what continent Armenia is on. At the same time, she also identified as a future wife and worried deeply about marrying. At age 20 she said: "I don't have a boyfriend. I've never had a boyfriend. I've never been asked out on a date, so

I'm kind of perplexed about that." She obsessed about her dating experience, expanding: "I actually have a count. I've been on twelve dates now. I technically was asked on three of them, but they were school functions where finally it had gotten to the point where there were these required dances and I had been to so many without a date, even though there were ten or so boys that didn't have a date, that finally the teachers went to them and said, 'Okay, one of you've got to ask her, sorry.' So I've been on that kind of date, but I don't count that as being asked on a date." Rhonda fretted about her few dates as she worried what they portended: life as a single woman. She maintained high levels of academic and institutional knowledge—resources she needed to become a professional—but also focused on using college to find a spouse.

Reba also displayed multiple identities in college, and, more broadly, in her time after high school. She first entered the military, hoping to become a journalist. Before the end of basic training her back gave out, and she was medically discharged. With her identity as a future military journalist thwarted, Reba turned to her other two identities—a rebel and a stay-at-home mom. She stopped pursuing a career and started living outside of institutions. She did not attend school or work and called herself an "extreme, almost alcoholic, always drinking, just obsessively every day." At age 19, she also married a high-school-educated soldier whom she met at a bar. She did not love him, but he provided a place to stay where she could drink and get high, and she had long identified as a future wife. Her marriage did not last long. She said her husband was controlling and did not allow her to display her former identity—to return to college and become a professional. Angry, Reba left him. She then enrolled in college and hoped to become a civilian journalist. However, once in college, she cycled back to rebelling as she broke rules and turned away from academics. She cashed her first $3,000 financial aid check and used it to buy cocaine. She used drugs, sold drugs, and skipped class. Within a year she was $13,000 in debt and nowhere close to earning a college degree.

Chris also displayed multiple identities in college: as a family man and artist. At the beginning of college, his father told him to become a responsible man who would earn enough to support a family. Already interested in becoming a family man, Chris followed his father's advice. He decided to become a nurse practitioner as it would allow him to provide for his future family while helping others. However, his relatively low levels of academic and institutional knowledge caught up with him. He struggled to understand his program's requirements and did not meet them. He also found the courses difficult. One semester, he failed every class but one.

In his effort to become a family man, Chris also looked for a spouse while in college. His tumultuous relationships distracted him from his courses. He began college living with his high school girlfriend. Their relationship was continuously fraught, and she cheated on Chris during their first semester of college. Their many fights and breakup took his focus away from school. As Chris put it, "Grade-wise, it really affected me." After a period of distress, Chris dated someone new. Within two months of dating his new girlfriend they moved in together, and a few months later they became engaged. They married a few years later when Chris was 22 years old. Their relationship again took his focus away from school. He loaned her his laptop when her father announced that they would go on a family vacation right before finals. Without his laptop, he failed his own final. His grades and ability to acquire academic knowledge were again impacted when his marriage dissolved: his wife came out as a lesbian, cheated on him, and asked Chris for a divorce.

As Chris's plans to become a young family man blew up, he returned to his other identity: becoming an artist. He left his nursing major and enrolled in two fine arts majors instead. He created art for social change and expressed an artists' disinterest in money—spending $7,000 from his savings on an art project. Each identity took Chris away from acquiring the resources he needed to stay in his class. His enactment of the family man identity took him away from acquiring the academic and institutional knowledge he needed to graduate from college in four years, and his artistic identity took him away from focusing on making economically prudent decisions. His non-accumulation of the resources associated with staying in the upper-middle class would portend his fall.

Life After College

As they left college and entered graduate school, work, and additional romantic relationships, explorers tried to maintain multiple identities. However, they found that pursuing one meant not acquiring the resources they needed to pursue another.

Rhonda always held two identities that would conflict when she became an adult. This issue came to a head as she left college. Rhonda enrolled in a prestigious master's degree program after graduating from college—a stepping-stone, she thought, to earning a PhD and becoming a professor. In her master's program she met an older doctoral student, a man who would become her husband. Rhonda was thrilled. After years of worrying about whether she would marry, she called her marriage her biggest accomplishment. In her conservative community, marrying young was prized, and she bragged that she was one of the first people from her high school class to marry. She had partially fulfilled an identity she had long desired.

Yet, after marrying, she began acting as a stay-at-home wife—an identity that would make it difficult for her to become a professional. After her first year of graduate school, Rhonda followed her husband to Europe for his year-long fellowship. There, she fell into a housewife role; her main job, she said, was grocery shopping. Once back in the United States, she learned that pursuing two identities had hurt her. She applied to doctoral programs but was rejected from all of them; she thought it was because she had not shown full devotion to a professional career. She explained: "[I] turned into this weird person who's in Europe and sending us applications, this weird person who didn't do anything last year." In addition, Rhonda felt that it might be too late to return to pursuing a professional job. Rhonda predicted that her husband would take two to four one-year post-docs, all in different locations, before applying for a professional job. She could not move with him and pursue her own career. This left her, at age 25, feeling that she had what she called a "fracturing of purpose" and "identity issues." She wanted to have multiple identities but had stopped acquiring the resources she needed to do so.[3]

Reba's life after college also left her without the resources she needed to become a professional. After leaving college the first time, Reba again cycled through her identities as a rebel, a stay-at-home wife, and a professional. Reba spent several years high on cocaine and then on meth, and dropped out of college to use drugs full time. After attending rehab and getting clean, Reba married her second husband, a police officer, and returned to identifying as a future stay-at-home mom. Her new goals were to have children, stay home with them, send them to college, and watch her children raise their own kids. However, Reba always wanted to explore multiple identities and she started to feel like marriage forced her into one. At age 28 she reflected: "I thought I was going to be happy as Suzy Homemaker. I thought I could make myself wanna do that. Two years ago I started realizing maybe this isn't right. A year ago, I was like, 'Oh no. What have I done? How can I correct this?'" She divorced her second husband and returned to college, hoping again to become a professional. Cycling through three identities meant that she was slow to acquire high levels of academic and institutional knowledge and slow to earn a college degree.

Chris's expression of multiple identities also left him behind those in his cohort. It took him eight years to graduate from college. With an artist's disinterest in money and the slow pathway he took through college, he graduated with $60,000 in student debt. He also did not prioritize earning money: "I think the thing that matters the least [in a job] is how much you make." He added: "I think you should do what you love. Hands down. If you don't do something that you're passionate about, it shows, and it erodes the rest of your life." Upon graduating from college, he took a job as a bus boy at a restaurant. He thought the job was perfect as it gave him time to do what he loved—create art. Of course, a low salary and a mountain of debt were not recipes for becoming a family man—an identity that, enacted in particular ways, could maintain his class position. Instead, as his two identities conflicted, Chris enacted the one that would, for the time being, put him on a downwardly mobile track.

Explorer Identities and Class Trajectories

The relationship between resources, explorer identities, and downward mobility varied based on the type of explorer. Women like Rhonda—women raised with high levels of academic and institutional knowledge in conservative communities—generally reproduced their class position. Their identities vacillated between a professional and stay-at-home mother. The first helped them maintain the resources they needed to stay in the upper-middle class through work and also positioned them to find upper-middle-class partners to marry. Thus, though some felt forced to give up one identity to pursue the other, either option would secure their class position. For example, at age 25, Rhonda was heartbroken that she was not in graduate school. She described it as a failure, an identity crisis, and a result of her early marriage and taking on the role of a stay-at-home wife. She instead worked for $10/hour in a retail shop, a job she did not enjoy. Still, she married a graduate student—someone who kept her in the upper-middle class. Whether she became a professional or married a professional in pursuit of becoming a professional herself, her class position would be secure.

Explorers like Reba were more often downwardly mobile. Raised with moderate levels of academic and institutional knowledge and enacting identities that did not demand the constant acquisition of resources, they tended to enter adulthood with college degrees but not professional jobs. Indeed, at

age 28, Reba worked in retail and was on the cusp of becoming a college graduate. After college ended, she wanted to live abroad but was unsure what job
she would take overseas. She was also open to not working but marrying and
becoming a stay-at-home mom.

Men like Chris—those raised with few resources and who identify as
family men and artists—were usually downwardly mobile as well. Their identities did not compel them to acquire the resources they were raised without
and they did not obtain them. Rather, most of these men, like Chris, graduated from college then found nonprofessional jobs. In short, most explorers
were downwardly mobile.[4]

The Surprise of Downward Mobility

Explorers rarely had a clear image of how their lives would turn out or how
their class trajectories would unfold. Still, as they entered adulthood, some
found themselves in a social class they did not expect. It is not hard to see
how their resources and identities took them away from the upper-middle
class. Why, then, did many of them not see it coming?

Explorers, like rebels and artists, experienced *life course change*. Early in
their lives, schools offered a variety of spaces to express their multiple identities. Courses prepared them to become professionals, extracurricular activities encouraged them to identify with the arts and athletics, schools provided
spaces to interact with romantic partners, and teachers offered rules against
which to rebel. As they left high school, they entered colleges, which had
the same organizational structure—courses, extracurricular activities, romantic spaces, and rules. Moreover, colleges admit youth with explorer identities and encourage students to maintain them. Their applications ask for
candidates committed to multiple pursuits and many colleges claim to help
students become even more well-rounded.[5] In the beginning of their lives,
explorer identities were tacitly and explicitly encouraged by the institutions
associated with maintaining a place in the upper-middle class.

Professional workplaces and marriage, however, do not provide as much
space for exploration. Both are what sociologists call "greedy institutions"—
ones that demand intensive time commitments.[6] These institutions are sufficiently consuming that they offer young adults little space to maintain
multiple identities. Indeed, Rhonda found that her marriage crowded out her
professional pursuits—and that the professional institutions she wanted to

enter offered little space to act as a devoted wife. Reba also found that her marriages crowded out her professional pursuits, but she was also hesitant to focus too much on professional pursuits unless they displaced her other identities. Chris, too, found that marriage was consuming. He needed to focus on acquiring high levels of academic and institutional knowledge if he were to stay in the upper-middle class, but his relationships diverted him. Thus, as they became adults, their explorer identities no longer neatly aligned with moving toward class reproduction. In fact, they could do the opposite as they left some youth opting out of professional work and marriage to pursue multiple identities.

Moving Forward

As they left their early adulthoods, explorers wanted to maintain their multiple identities. Rhonda hoped to find a way to integrate her professional identity with her stay-at-home mother identity, but she was not sure it was possible. She reluctantly started to imagine herself as a mom and a dental hygienist. Married to a professional, she would maintain her class position but not be the person she long wanted to be.[7]

Reba left her early adulthood committed to remaining an explorer. At age 28, she maintained: "I do have [a sense of purpose] on the most basic level. My purpose here is to do a lot of different things." She might travel abroad as an English teacher, a nongovernmental worker, or volunteer coordinator. Or she might meet someone, marry, and not work. She was open to what possibilities arose and was more committed to exploring than maintaining her class position. She thought she would not only be a professional, saying: "I've really gotten away from the idea of wanting to have some sort of career." Instead she would evaluate her life through the lens of an explorer. A good life was one in which she could reflect and say, "Overall it was a really good ride."

Chris could imagine his future unfolding in multiple directions. He considered moving to a big city to pursue a professional job as an illustrator but also considered remaining in a working-class job that would allow him to pursue his artwork on his own. He also wanted to marry and have children in the next five years and to raise his kids in a financially stable home. Doing so might motivate him to find a professional job—one he could obtain given his college degree—or he could frame providing as simply having a steady job. In general, explorers' future trajectories were the most uncertain. They had many possibilities ahead of them, and their futures may be likely to resemble the zigzagging of their pasts. Though some might give up one part of their identity to focus on another, others were likely to lead a life of flux, flexibility, and exploration—a life that did not put them on a straight path toward a particular class location.

8

Exceptions

In the majority of cases, inherited resources and identities aligned to create mobility pathways. Those with inherited resource strengths and professional identities reproduced their childhood class position, while those with inherited resource weaknesses and most other identities entered downwardly mobile trajectories.[1] But this pattern leaves us with a key question: Is downward mobility only the result of inherited resources *or* identities or do both play a meaningful role? This chapter answers this question by focusing on the mobility trajectories of two groups: youth with identities that did not map onto their inherited resources, and youth whose inherited resources or identities changed. In doing so, it shows that both inherited resources and identities relate to upper-middle-class youth's mobility pathways.

Resource-Identity Misalignments

Perhaps the clearest way to understand whether both inherited resources and identities are associated with downward mobility is to examine the cases in which they are misaligned. If only inherited resources were associated with downward mobility, then regardless of youths' identity, youth with inherited resource strengths would avoid downward mobility. This is not what the data show. Instead, as the columns of Table 8.1 display, among youth raised with inherited resource strengths, 4% with professional identities were on downwardly mobile trajectories but far more—43%—with nonprofessional identities were on the same trajectory. Similarly, if inherited resource weaknesses alone were associated with downward mobility, we would see similar amounts of downward mobility regardless of youth's identities. This is also not what the data show. Among youth with inherited resource weaknesses, there was also a big divide by identity: 31% of youth with professional identities were on downwardly mobile trajectories while far more—74%—of youth with nonprofessional identities were on the same trajectory. These large

Privilege Lost. Jessi Streib, Oxford University Press (2020) © Oxford University Press.
DOI: 10.1093/oso/9780190854041.001.0001

Table 8.1 Inherited Resources, Identities, and the Number and Percent of Downwardly Mobile Respondents

	Resource Strengths	Resource Weaknesses
Professional Identity	1/27 (4%)	4/13 (31%)
Nonprofessional Identity	6/14 (43%)	39/53 (74%)

differences indicate that inherited resources alone did not shape mobility trajectories. Identities relate to mobility too.

We can take the same approach to understanding if identities shape downward mobility alone. If this were the case, we would see similar rates of downward mobility for youth with the same identities, regardless of their inherited resources. Again, this is not what the data show. As displayed in the rows of Table 8.1, among youth with professional identities, 4% with inherited resource strengths entered downwardly mobile trajectories compared to 31% with inherited resource weaknesses. Among youth with nonprofessional identities, 43% with inherited resource strengths entered downwardly mobile trajectories compared to 74% with inherited resource weaknesses. These gaps suggest that identities do not shape mobility trajectories on their own either. Knowing both youth's inherited resources and their identity tells us far more about which mobility pathway they are likely to take.

For upper-middle-class youth with resource-identity mismatches, what mattered more for their mobility trajectory—their inherited resources or their identities? It often varied by person according to the strength of their inherited resources and identities. Some youth had such dramatic inherited resource strengths or weaknesses that they would shape their mobility trajectories no matter their identity. Other youth had such strongly held identities that they would shape their mobility paths no matter their inherited resources.

This chapter spotlights four youth with resource-identity mismatches to show how both inherited resources and identities relate to mobility. It begins with youth whose identities divert them from the mobility trajectories their resources placed them on then moves to youth whose resources divert them from the pathways their identities moved them toward. Next, the chapter examines youth whose inherited resources or identities changed dramatically. Doing so shows how identities can lead youth toward or away from their original social class, regardless of their resources.

The Primacy of Identities

Travis and Vana were among the quarter of the sample whose identities did not neatly follow from their inherited resources. Travis was raised with re-source strengths but did not develop a sole professional or family man identity. Despite his great family resources, without one of these identities, he entered a downwardly mobile trajectory. Vana's situation was the oppo-site: she was raised with resource weaknesses yet developed a professional identity. Despite her family's few resources, her identity propelled her to stay in the upper-middle class. Their stories highlight that inherited resources do not determine mobility pathways alone. Identities can reroute them.

Travis

Travis's story highlights how identities can push youth toward downward mobility even when they inherit many resources. Travis was a tall young man with short brown hair and child-like eyes. He grew up in a privileged Christian family in the American South. His parents both held bachelor's degrees and professional jobs, and their combined income put them in the study's highest income bracket. Travis also felt close to both of his parents and regularly talked with them about school, college, work, relationships, and sports. Travis recognized he had many advantages and even wondered if they were too much. Would he work harder if his parents did not have so much money? Would he be happier if his parents offered him less advice?

With inherited resource strengths and living in a conservative community, it was likely that Travis would identify as a family man and use his inherited resources to reproduce his class position. But Travis never felt solely like a family man. Instead, he felt like an explorer: part family man, part athlete, and part rebel.

In high school, Travis identified as a family man and an athlete. Asked what he was most enthusiastic about, he answered by naming his goals of becoming a married man and provider: "Getting grown up and getting mar-ried. Getting paid." Asked what job he wanted, he replied that he did not know: any job that paid well would do. At the same time, Travis identified as an athlete. He starred on his high school's basketball team, felt that his peers looked up to him for his athletic abilities, and dreamed of playing basketball in college.

Enacting these identities required that Travis take particular approaches—but not that he acquire the resources he needed to maintain his inherited resource strengths. In high school, Travis enacted his family man identity, in part, by dating seriously. At age 15, he started a relationship with a girl he thought he would marry; he felt deeply committed to her during their two-plus year relationship. Travis also enacted his athlete identity. When not with his girlfriend, he was often in the gym or with his team. Neither of these focuses involved maintaining high levels of academic knowledge, and his approach to schoolwork did not either. Though his parents instructed him to focus on his grades, Travis believed he only needed good enough grades to be the person he wanted to be—someone who would obtain a steady job and who was eligible to play basketball in college.

Travis attended college. There, he maintained identities that did not encourage him to preserve high levels of resources. He continued, in part, to act like a family man. At age 19, asked what made him most sad or depressed, he talked of missing a component of the family man identity: "Not having a girlfriend to be with." Asked about his main goal, he stayed on the same theme: "Find true love." At age 22, when Travis described his idea of a good life, he talked of becoming a family man: "Getting married and have a kid or two. Having them grow up and do good. Have a couple of grandkids." Trying to meet his goal, he dated often, moving in and out of long-term relationships. He also did not focus on his academic work. Youth who identified as family men saw work as a means to an end rather than an end in itself. He enacted that identity by treating his academic work in the same way. At best, he thought he should raise his grades enough to remain in college. Beyond that, he saw studying as unimportant.

Travis did not only feel like a family man while in college but held other identities as well. He entered college identifying as an athlete, but that identity faded after a fight with his coach got him kicked off the basketball team. He then developed a new identity. He would look back on his college years and recall, "I was a little rebel." He stole from stores; was arrested for driving under the influence; partied constantly; and, when not in a relationship, slept with dozens of women, including women who were married and engaged. The archetype of the rebel also includes rejecting academic work, and Travis followed this aspect of the model as well. As he put it at age 19, "If I need to do some homework, I'd go to a party." He found it difficult "not to party your life away." He also ignored his mother when she advised him to study more; he preferred to party instead.

Of course, enacting his identities in college—especially the rebel identity—left him with little academic and institutional knowledge compared with his peers born into the upper-middle class. He failed courses, was put on academic probation, and failed again. He selected majors but switched often. Not having maintained high levels of cultural resources by researching majors and jobs, he was repeatedly surprised that the majors he chose and that his parents chose for him did not lead to the types of jobs he expected. In all, he was kicked out of at least two colleges, tried at least three majors, and attended four universities before earning a bachelor's degree.

Upon leaving college, Travis had few options for remaining in the upper-middle class. He did not have the level of academic or institutional knowledge needed to enter many professional jobs, nor did he have the interest in gaining it or trying to proceed without it. He worked as a nursing assistant in college and kept that job after he graduated. His mother sent him job ads for professional positions, but he rarely applied to them. He admitted: "I could probably be a lot more motivated in finding a job and applying to jobs and getting my résumé a lot better." Instead, Travis focused on becoming one of the people he long wanted to be: a married man and provider. A few years after graduating college, he proposed to his girlfriend of a year—a nurse whom he met at the hospital where they each worked. He looked forward to a life of marriage, raising children, and teaching them to play basketball. For the moment, at least, he was content acting as a family man—even, or especially, a nonprofessional one.

Travis's life is an example of how identities can override inherited resources in charting class trajectories. Travis inherited many resources, but his identities gave him little reason to maintain them. His identities told him what goals to desire—a steady job (family man), improbable job (athlete), or no job (rebel). Enacting identities also came with approaches—ones that varied from treating schoolwork as a means to an end (family man) to rejecting it altogether (rebel). Without an identity that led him to desire a professional job or to maintain the resource advantages his parents initially provided, he would not stay in the upper-middle class. At age 27, he was on a downwardly mobile trajectory and had no plans to reverse course.

Vana

Vana's story also shows that identities can change mobility trajectories—in her case, pulling her toward class reproduction despite her inherited resource weaknesses. Vana, a self-depreciating young woman who wore sweatpants, plain T-shirts, and, once, a bandana to her interviews, was raised on the edge of the upper-middle class—situated there more by a technicality than by her family's resources. Her parents divorced when she was young, and Vana visited her father, a mechanic, only once or twice a year. Vana was primarily raised by her mother, who worked as a teacher before becoming an administrative assistant and then a seamstress.

Vana described receiving few resources from her parents, who she experienced as hands-off. Growing up, Vana talked to her father on the phone every week; he offered her advice when she asked for it but not when she didn't. Vana was closer to her mother, but as Vana believed her mother was emotionally unstable, Vana did not think she was in a position to help her with schoolwork or prepare her for the future. Furthermore, Vana's parents had little money for those technically in the upper-middle class—a teacher's and mechanic's salary only went so far.

Vana was then raised with three resource weaknesses—receiving less human, cultural, and economic resources from her parents than most of her peers who grew up in the upper-middle class. Nevertheless, she developed a professional identity—one often associated with growing up with resource strengths. She expressed the components of the professional identity, viewing schoolwork as intrinsically interesting, striving for a sense of achievement, and putting long hours into schoolwork. She said of herself: "I'm a complete nerd. I like to learn." She added: "I tend to feel [at home] around intellectuals—other people who really like to understand or to think about things." She also strove for recognizable achievements, revealing: "The things that make me really happy seem to involve other people's recognition of my achievements." When asked what it would mean not to live a good life, she again emphasized achievement: "Someone who didn't accomplish anything."

Vana entered college with a professional identity—one that would help her turn her inherited resource weaknesses into acquired resource strengths. Though she described her parents as unable to help her gain academic knowledge, with a professional identity she was motivated to acquire it through her university. She described one of her first college courses: "I took a survey course in engineering, and I utterly loved it and was just utterly fascinated by how all these different areas of science come together." Hooked by the course, she expressed her professional identity by throwing herself into the field and building her human capital. She spent much of her time in college drawing blueprints, designing sequences, and learning to use lab equipment. Eager to express her professional identity, she also went to her university's career center to learn how to find professional jobs. With their help, she found three internships with the top companies in her field and developed what she considered to be a fantastic résumé. Moreover, she maintained her acquired resources and identity throughout personal crises—she took care of her mother when she struggled with severe mental health issues and stayed focused on her schoolwork through her own clinical depression.

Vana persevered, and after graduating from college having thrown herself into her schoolwork, she threw herself into paid work. She became a professional engineer and dedicated herself to the job—moving twice for new job opportunities in different states, feeling that work consumed her life, and admitting: "I focused on my job so much that I've missed out on a lot." As part of commitment to work, Vana accumulated the academic skills and cultural knowledge she needed to remain a professional and become a higher status one. She explained: "I'm gathering experience and gathering credentials for bigger, better things." She hoped to enter a specialist lab—a job that would reflect her professional identity and maintain her position as a professional. She described: "Ideally I'd like to be somewhere that I get to play in a lab.[2] I love that stuff. I think it's so awesome to really understand what's going on. The heat, the electricity, and getting down in there and figuring out what the atoms are doing. I'm such a freakin' nerd. I love that stuff. And I'd like nothing better than to be around it all the time."

Aligned with the professional identity, Vana also put off marriage. Her career kept her on the move and in the lab, making it difficult to meet potential partners.[3] At age 28, she was single. She hoped to marry in the future and to maintain her professional identity—an identity that drove her to transform her early resource weaknesses into later resource strengths. Armed with this identity, she remained in the upper-middle class as a young adult.

The Primacy of Resources

Just as identities could push youth with inherited resource strengths toward downward mobility and pull youth with inherited resource weaknesses toward class reproduction, inherited resources could also change mobility pathways that seemed governed by identities. This was particularly the case for youth raised with resource strengths as their inherited resources could lower the costs of a nonprofessional identity. This occurred in two ways. First, inherited resource strengths provided some youth with a sufficiently high starting point that they could afford not to focus on acquiring more resources and still retain enough to remain in the upper-middle class. This occurred in the case of several stay-at-home mothers and family men, including Rebecca and Terrence, whose stories were told in chapters 3 and 4. Second, inherited resource strengths could serve as a safety net. When youth's nonprofessional identities took them toward a lower social class, their inherited resources could bounce them back to the upper-middle class. The second occurred in the case of Kendra, whose story is told next.

Kendra

Kendra was a short woman with wavy brown hair and fair skin. She inherited considerable resource strengths. Her graduate-school-educated mother owned a professional services firm, her graduate-school-educated father worked in real estate and finance, and her family employed a long-term nanny whom Kendra considered to be a second mother. She talked to her family regularly about school, college, and work; they gave her advice about how to succeed in each. At age 17, she said of her parents: "They're both extremely supportive with my goals with college or school or what I want to do—extremely supportive in school and academics." Kendra's parents were also in the study's highest income bracket—$100,000 or above. With this money, Kendra's parents could afford to live in a well-off neighborhood and send Kendra to private school from kindergarten through college. Kendra then grew up surrounded by privileged people, so much so that she was well into her teenage years before she realized that not everyone attended college.

Kendra's inherited resources predicted that she would identify as a professional and reproduce her class position. Instead, Kendra identified as an artist—a creative worker in a winner-takes-all field. In high school she thought she would become a journalist or photographer. In college, she refined her plan, deciding she wanted to become a writer for nationally aired television shows. Kendra's goals were grand, but as she put it, "I'm not a type of person who's okay not being in the limelight."

Like other artists, Kendra's plan for meeting her goals was to invest in her skills and then assume a job would follow. In high school she studied hard and practiced her writing skills as her yearbook's editor. In college, she majored in English to further develop her relevant skills, and also wrote for one of her college's magazine. Yet, like other artists, Kendra expressed disinterest in learning about the labor market. Despite her research skills and connections, she misunderstood basic facts about work. For instance, she did not realize that not every interview would lead to a job. She learned this the hard way after she applied for a second internship:

> Sophomore summer, getting the internship was a breeze, and I thought that was the typical way it happens. You apply for something, you're qualified, you're good, we notice you, you're hired. Literally I met with the HR person and she scheduled a meeting with someone, a producer, in the production/ development department, and the next thing I know, that afternoon I had the job. So what happened was spring semester, junior year, when I was applying for jobs, I got a fair amount of interviews but never a job. I had these breakdowns where I'd be bawling in front of my dad, and he'd say, "Kendra, this is life." [I responded] "I don't understand! Real life was everything worked out for me. What do you mean this is real life? This is not how it's supposed to happen!"

Kendra learned that not every interview would lead to a job, but her new insight did not lead her to question her other assumptions or research how to find jobs in her field. Instead, she continued to express disinterest in the labor market, even chiding her college peers for focusing on how to earn money.[4] After graduating from college, she moved to a city with jobs for television writers and looked for work. She did not realize that becoming a writer for television shows was unlikely to occur in a winner-takes-all market.

Kendra's work experience was then predictable for the market she entered, though unpredictable to her. She entered a field with project-based jobs, strict hierarchies, and where most people who want to become professional writers fail to do so. Her work experience reflected this labor market. She spent six years flitting from job to job, usually quitting after she realized that her current company would not promote her to a writing role. She did not hold a single job for more than eight months, and, other than a few scripts that a theater and an online channel picked up, she had few writing successes. Having not researched the labor market, she found her experiences surprising and distressing. Kendra explained: "I was just really depressed that my writing wasn't really happening, that wasn't my job, that I'm so subservient to my bosses. It's almost like you're just a paid laborer, like 'Get me lunch, get me coffee, get me this.' And I felt like I was nothing, like I was of no importance, and like my education didn't mean anything." Claiming to be clinically depressed after years of trying and failing to become a television writer and producer, Kendra eventually decided it was not healthy to continue to pursue her dream. At age 27, she returned to her parents' house without a professional career or a résumé filled with accomplishments.

At age 27, Kendra not only had not found a professional job but also had not found a professional spouse. She had always viewed marriage as happening after she started her writing career. At age 22, she expressed: "I'm really professionally driven, career driven. I'm still focused a lot on that. Having a husband is not a priority in my life right now." At age 27, she still felt that putting off relationships was the right call, asking out loud: "Why would you prioritize something [like relationships] that's so fleeting and maybe wouldn't go anywhere whereas you could work to secure a job and education?" Feeling so strongly about the need for a career to come before marriage, Kendra had only one romantic relationship ever—a long-distance one that fizzled out before she got to know him.

Thus, at age 27, Kendra had not maintained her early resource strengths. Her record of human capital accumulation was lower than that of her peers; she had never held a steady job where she could advance her skills. Her record of cultural capital accumulation was also thin; she had a limited understanding of how to navigate the labor market. Her economic capital was low as well, as her work experience was sparse. Yet, despite her de-accumulation of resources, Kendra remained in the upper-middle class. After Kendra gave up on becoming a television writer, her mother offered her a job at the firm she owned and managed. Kendra took it. The job kept her in the upper-middle class by providing her a professional position. However, Kendra still identified as an artist and yearned to give writing another try. Nevertheless, for the time being, her mother's resources provided a safety net. She could stay in the upper-middle class despite that her identity led her to lose her early resource advantages.

The Indirect Importance of Resource Weaknesses

Could inherited resource weaknesses pull down the mobility trajectories of youth with professional identities just as inherited resource strengths could boost the mobility trajectories of youth with nonprofessional identities? If the answer were a straightforward yes, we would see stories of youth with professional identities whose low levels of economic resources prevented them from attending college or whose dedication to schoolwork and learning to navigate institutions was not enough to catch up to their peers. These stories are not in the data—perhaps because they are unlikely to happen to upper-middle-class youth. Upper-middle-class youth who have fewer resources than their upper-middle-class peers still tend to have more resources than most Americans.

Instead, inherited resources weaknesses could play an indirect role in shaping professionally identified youth's mobility trajectories. This indirect route went through youth's identities, as not all youth with inherited resource weaknesses enacted the same identity as their peers with inherited resource strengths. The four youth with inherited resource weaknesses, professional identities, and downwardly mobile trajectories enacted only a partial professional identity. They either set professional goals but did not realize that they needed to act like a professional to meet them or they acted like a professional but directed their efforts toward becoming a nonprofessional: becoming a paramedic, nurse, or manager at a retail store. As only youth with inherited resource weaknesses enacted this partial-professional identity,[5] it is likely that inherited resources played a role in shaping their identity, and, in turn, in shaping their mobility trajectory.

Trey was one of the youths with a partial-professional identity. He was a shy and slender youth with curly black hair who was raised in a heartland suburb. His parents offered him few resources. His father was a college-educated accountant, but Trey said he rarely interacted with him. At age 17, Trey explained: "He pretty much just leaves us alone and lets us do what we want." Trey's mother was a college-educated stay-at-home mother before taking a customer services job. She, too, was hands-off. As he described: "I talked to her for about thirty minutes yesterday, and I probably hadn't talked to her the rest of this week." Their minimal interactions were not unusual. Asked if he missed his mother after she transitioned from being a stay-at-home mother to working, Trey said: "It doesn't really matter. I never really talked to her that much in the first place." Moreover, Trey's parents had relatively low incomes for the upper-middle class—about $55,000 a year combined. They had also not saved for Trey to attend college, using their disposable income to send his older sister to college instead.

Despite inheriting relatively few resources, Trey thought of himself as a future professional. At age 15, he wanted to become a video game designer.

At age 17, he gave up that idea for a new professional plan: he wanted to become a mechanical engineer who made medical devices for hospitals. He held onto this plan for at least the next eight years, seeing himself as a future professional.

However, while Trey had professional aspirations, he did not enact the professional identity to its full extent and did not acquire additional resources. Having inherited limited human and cultural resources, he did not understand that he needed to acquire more resources to meet his goals. Thus, unlike professionals who dedicated themselves to academic work, strove for a sense of accomplishment, and found schoolwork intrinsically interesting, Trey instead viewed school as simply an institution to pass through. At age 15, he had the following conversation with his interviewer:

INTERVIEWER: How much do you care about doing well at school?
TREY: Not all that much. Just need to pass, that's it.
INTERVIEWER: Do you think that it's not too important then?
TREY: No, not really.
INTERVIEWER: Why not?
TREY: I think you just need to get the gist of what they're teaching, that's it.

At age 17, Trey still did not have the inherited resources to understand that becoming a professional meant acting like one from an early age. Rather, at age 17, he did not see the need to dedicate himself to acquiring academic knowledge. He said: "I think [grades are] important to get into college. But other than that, I don't think it's that important." He added: "Some of the classes that I take, some of them I don't worry that much about, so I don't try hard." Despite wanting to become an engineer, Trey put his math courses into this category. He thought only aviation engineers needed to understand math; he did not have the cultural resources to know that mechanical engineers use math as well.

Trey then attended an engineering college with the hopes of becoming a mechanical engineer. However, he lacked both the inherited and acquired resources to know how to succeed. Having entered college only getting the "gist" of his high school courses, he fell behind in his college courses. He did not know how to recover. Rather than enacting a professional identity by devoting himself to coursework, he turned to extracurricular pursuits instead: he devoted 40 hours a week to a non-academic campus competition. He viewed this time as productive, believing that winning would look good on his résumé. No one seemed to tell him that winning an extracurricular competition would mean little if he did not pass his classes. Indeed, two years into college, Trey was put on academic probation after failing several classes. He appealed the decision but was not allowed to return.

Trey left college but continued to hold onto his professional goals. At age 20, he became a cashier at a grocery store and held that job for the next five years. During this time, he planned to return to college, major in engineering, and then complete a doctoral degree in engineering. Trey did not take any steps to enact his plan. He did not study calculus on his own after failing calculus repeatedly. He also did not research programs that would accept him or learn more about what it took to become an engineer. Raised with resource weaknesses, his professional identity was always partial—not strong enough to encourage him to acquire the resources he was raised without. Without these resources, he did not become a young professional. Instead, he continued to work as a cashier, and was, for the time being, downwardly mobile.

Change

The importance of inherited resources and identities can also be understood through cases in which either inherited resources or identities changed while the other did not. In these cases, youth's identities were initially aligned with their inherited resources but became misaligned as one changed without the other. If a youth's mobility pathway remained stable after their resources changed but not their identity, this would indicate that their identity mattered in their mobility trajectory. If a youth's mobility pathway remained stable after their identity changed but not their inherited resources, this would indicate that their inherited resources mattered more than their identity in shaping their mobility trajectory.

There were few cases of substantial changes in youth's inherited resources or identities. In this study, only one professional youth's inherited resources dramatically changed while their identity remained the same, and only three youth replaced their nonprofessional identities with professional ones. In the former case, the loss of family resources did not change his mobility trajectory. In the latter cases, the change from rebel to professional—even with no change in inherited resources—related to youth's jump from downwardly mobile trajectories to class reproduction ones. Each case highlights the importance of identities in shaping mobility trajectories. When a change occurred, youth's mobility trajectory was better aligned with their identity than their resources.

In addition, we can examine cases when professionals' inherited resources *and* identities changed. In these cases, which were also rare, youth lost the resources associated with their identity and then their identity changed as well. When this occurred, both resource loss and identity change worked together to move youth who were on class reproduction tracks to downwardly mobile ones. These youth's stories tell us that both inherited resources and identities relate to mobility pathways, but that inherited resources often work through identities.

Luke

Luke's case was the only one of identity stability during inherited resource change among youth who identified as professionals.[6] Luke was a laid-back, confident teen who grew up in a liberal community with his father, a small-business owner with some college experience, and his mother, a teacher with a master's degree. Both of his parents were hands-on, with his father especially so. Luke described his father as his best friend and a good source of advice: "My dad just knows so much about everything." He also was close to his mother, saying that she knew him well and that they talked all the time. His parents also earned over $100,000 a year, putting them in the top 20% of Americans' household incomes at the time.[7]

Unsurprisingly given his resources and community, Luke grew up identifying as a professional. He long assumed he would take over his father's business and considered becoming a politician. In high school he acted the part of a young professional. Asked about the biggest challenge for teenagers, he replied with an academic concern: "College, definitely. Especially going to a real good college. Especially in the town I live in, it's just all about college. It's all about the SAT scores, college, that kind of stuff." Accordingly, he made sure to keep his grades high enough to be accepted by a selective college and to talk to professionals about which college to attend.

Luke attended college and continued to receive resources from his family. His parents paid for his tuition, and he talked to his father three times a day—receiving advice about many aspects of his life.[8] Then, early in his college career, Luke's father died unexpectedly. Luke lost his father—his best friend, main source of advice, and main source of economic resources.

Yet, Luke said of his father's death, "It hasn't necessarily affected my life that much. I haven't had to make any changes really." Identifying as a professional, he found other ways to maintain his early resource strengths. He took out student loans to cover his college costs. He sought advice from other sources. His sister was four years older than him, and Luke turned to her and her boyfriend for advice about navigating college. He also had an aunt and uncle, former coach, and his father's business partner whom he looked to for academic and career advice. He also kept up his academic knowledge. He studied for his classes with his fraternity brothers and took political science courses to prepare for a potential career in politics. His father's death also led him to use and develop more skills: while still in college, Luke learned to read lawyers' and accountants' documents when he took charge of aspects of his father's business. Determined to retain and acquire the resources he needed to remain a professional, Luke did not let his resources slip.

Maintaining high levels of resources even though his main source of them disappeared, Luke remained on a class reproduction track. After graduating from college, he took over his father's business. He then left for law school, graduated, and gave up the family business for a public relations job with a political think tank. Like other professionals, he had put off dating until after his career was set; at age 27 he had not had a relationship that lasted for more than a few months. Still, he reproduced his class position on his own. His identity helped him do so because it kept him focused on obtaining resources he needed to stay ahead.

Mitch

Mitch was one of three respondents who replaced a nonprofessional identity with a professional one. Unlike explorers, these respondents did not rotate between identities or hold several identities simultaneously, but thoroughly rid themselves of one identity and became a new type of person. The three respondents each originally identified as a rebel. After learning of the high costs of their identity—through a warning sign, a rape, and, respectively, a month-long hospital stay—they ditched their rebel identities to become professionals. In each case, when they changed identities, they changed mobility pathways, even though they did not inherit new resources.

Mitch was a funny and laid-back young man who was built like a football player. He grew up with his mother, a nurse with an associate's degree, and his father, a small-business owner with a bachelor's degree. Mitch grew up close to his mother. As a teenager, he said: "We communicate. We tell each other pretty much everything. She knows everything about me." However, it was Mitch's father, not his mother, who was best positioned to provide Mitch with academic and institutional knowledge, and Mitch said his father did not take on this role. Mitch explained: "Me and my dad don't talk." He continued: "[My dad] keeps to himself a lot . . . He doesn't really talk a lot."

Not surprisingly given Mitch's inherited resources, he initially identified as a rebel. He broke many rules. He started smoking pot during his first year of high school and smoked several times a day throughout his high school career. He got in fights, once even kicking in the doors, ripping off the windshield wipers, and smashing in the taillights of a rival's car while his rival was in it. He stole money from his college savings account to buy and sell steroids. He lied to his parents, and, one day, came home so belligerently drunk that his parents called the police, who, in turn, handcuffed him. Eventually, his parents kicked him out of the house, telling Mitch he needed a wake-up call.

Throughout this time, Mitch acted like a rebel at school. He talked back to teachers and coaches. He attended his classes high. He failed a number of classes. As a senior, he needed to take a summer course to make up for a course he failed. He decided not to attend—getting high sounded better than finishing his degree. At age 18, Mitch was a high school dropout with a GED. He worked as a janitor.

But then, at age 19, Mitch began to change. He moved back in with his parents and his uncle moved in too. Mitch's uncle provided him with an example of how his life would unfold as a rebel. Mitch contemplated: "Do I like where my life's headed? No, 'cause my life's headed like my uncle's: sleeping in a car and stealing from a church." Mitch continued: "[I'm] a little worried that I'm going to end up like both of my uncles, working $15 an hour jobs when I'm fucking thirty-eight, thirty-five years old. I know I'm better than that. So I've got to get my shit together so it will be better than that."

Mitch's uncle showed Mitch that his identity could be costly—leading to a life in a lower social class. Mitch vowed to become a new person. He stopped smoking pot entirely and stopped hanging out with his friends that did. He enrolled in community college and started to take school seriously; he liked that he could choose his own college courses, and no one told him where to be. He then transferred to a four-year college and committed himself to studying. He also began to reach out to his father more often, seeking his advice about college and work. By the end of his senior year, he was the top-ranked student in his major.

When he graduated from college, Mitch identified and worked as a professional. In college, he interned with a prominent company and was asked to stay on as a business information specialist when he graduated. Like other professionals, he found joy in his work: "I go into work every day and I love it." Like professionals, he also invested in maintaining his newly acquired resources so that he could stay ahead. Mitch explained: "Currently if I had to say what I'm living for or what my passion would be is to just create a foundation, to make sure that I'm gaining skills and different abilities and working my way to be able to have an understanding." He continued to talk of building his academic and cultural resources: "If you put in the time and you really understand the business and you understand the systems that you're working with and you can put in five to seven years there, you can put that on your résumé and you can go a lot of other places and do very, very well." He planned to return to school to receive an MBA and then to take over his father's business or move up in the business world.

Mitch then made a relatively quick transition from rebel to professional. As a rebel, Mitch was a high school dropout who worked as a janitor. Once he began to act like a professional, he acquired a new set of human and cultural capital and then became a college-educated professional. Importantly, his family resources never changed; they could not be responsible for the change in his mobility path. But his identity did change, and after his identity changed his mobility path did too. For Mitch, his new professional identity directed him to gain academic and cultural knowledge and to use it toward gaining a professional job.

Tori

Tori was a tall, thin, modest woman who had a difficult life for a youth born into the upper-middle class. She was raised by both parents, but her stable family life did not last long. When she was nine years old, the police showed up at Tori's house to arrest her father for domestic violence. Her parents then divorced. It was the first time her resources were taken away. Tori moved out of the house that her father's paycheck afforded and into a one-room apartment with her mother and two siblings. She learned to wash clothes by hand because they did not have a washer and dryer.

Tori's family's poverty did not last long. Her mother returned to college then quickly rose through the ranks at work. Soon she was a high-powered and highly paid analyst, and Tori was living in a five-bedroom three-car-garage house in the suburbs. In this environment, Tori identified as a professional. As she put it, "Up until my senior year [of high school], I was very high achieving and identified myself with those achievements." She was in the running for high school valedictorian; a member of the National Honors Society and student council; president of one of her school's academic clubs; and told that she was expected to go far professionally. She took for granted that she would become a college graduate and have a professional career.

Yet, as Tori spent her final years at home, her inherited resources changed again. Her mother began dating someone new and then married him. Tori's stepfather refused to talk to Tori, and her mother stopped talking to Tori too. The human and cultural resources she once received from her mother stopped flowing, and her father was still not part of her life.

Close to completing high school, Tori graduated then left for college. There, she mourned the loss of her mother, who she described as having pushed her away. She also mourned the loss of her friend, who died in a car crash soon after Tori arrived at college. It was too much for her to take. Tori turned off her cell phone, put it in a drawer, and climbed into bed. She stayed there for most of her first months at college. Not attending classes, she failed them all.

Tori emerged from her depression a new person. Though she was raised with minimal exposure to religion, she appreciated what she had observed and decided to join a conservative Christian church. The church became the main fixture in her life—the pastor's wife served as a motherly figure, and the congregation provided her with many friends. She became the type of person the church rewarded: she began to identify as a stay-at-home mother.

By age 23, Tori fully identified as a stay-at-home mother and gave up her idea of becoming a professional. She said of her future: "The ideal is to stay at home with my kids if we could financially do it." At age 28, she maintained this idea of herself. She listed her highest priorities: "Building a strong family, marrying the right person, having a strong marriage. If I am able to have children, that I nurture them . . . Outside of that, everything else would be a bonus." With this new identity, she also gave up her professional goals. When a distant cousin offered her a job doing secretarial and organizational work for a retirement community, she jumped on the opportunity. She imagined she would stay in this job until becoming a stay-at-home mom.

At age 28, Tori was then no longer the person she was as a teenager, nor was she on the mobility track she had once been on. A change in her inherited resources triggered an identity change. She replaced an identity bolstered by high levels of resources with an identity that made a virtue out of lacking the resources she no longer had. Without the resources associated with staying in the upper-middle class or an identity oriented toward acquiring new resources, Tori fell out of the upper-middle class. She would not become the young professional she once imagined but became a working-class future stay-at-home mother instead.

Conclusion

This chapter showed that both youths' identities and inherited resources correspond to their mobility trajectories. Identities were closely associated with mobility paths. They pushed youth with inherited resource strengths not to maintain them and to fall out of the upper-middle class; they also pushed youth with inherited resource weaknesses to acquire resource strengths and remain in the upper-middle class. At the same time, inherited resources related to mobility too. They prevented youth with nonprofessional identities from falling too far, allowed youth who had fallen to rise back into the upper-middle class, and related to changes in identities and then to changes in mobility paths.

It should not be surprising that both inherited resources and identities coincided with upper-middle-class youth's mobility trajectories. Inherited resources can never work alone; identities tell youth if and how to use them. Identities cannot be viewed apart from inherited resources; inherited resources shape the consequences of identities. And, of course, resources always play a role in mobility—sometimes acquired resources just play a larger role than inherited ones. Downward mobility from the upper-middle class then typically relates both to resource weaknesses—inherited, acquired, or both—and to nonprofessional identities.

Of course, this chapter also raises a new question: Why do some youth have identities that map onto their resources and communities while others do not? Though the data do not provide definitive answers, it likely relates to dimensions of youth's resources and communities that go beyond human, cultural, and economic resources in liberal or conservative communities. Other relevant resources include physical characteristics such as height and appearance—ones that likely matter for the ability to gain status by being an athlete or stay-at-home mother. The (in)ability to learn academic information quickly—regardless of what happens at home—may also relate to the identities youth adopt. The human and cultural capital youth inherit may also matter but be mis-measured for some. Some parents' resources do not correspond well to their educations and occupations, and some youth may have such hands-on teachers or caregivers that their parents' resources become less important.

A broader understanding of communities may help us understand youth's identities as well. Communities are not only liberal or conservative but have local status systems. Families, schools, peer groups, extracurricular communities, and charismatic community leaders model and value some identities over others, and each may relate to which identity youth adopt. Family dynamics—such as whether an older sibling or parent is admired or disdained—may also create incentives for youth to be similar or different than those around them. Likewise, youth's other identities may matter as well. For instance, gay and lesbian youth born in the 1980s may have been particularly likely to identify as explorers. Their ability to gain status through family and through work were not guaranteed, so being open to multiple identities may have seemed like a safer bet.

In addition, this chapter raises questions about why some youth change identities after their resources change while others do not. It's not clear why Luke maintained his identity when his resources changed while Tori did not maintain hers. It may be that Luke had more opportunities to maintain his resource advantages from sources outside of his father, while Tori had fewer places to turn. She did not have older siblings or aunts and uncles to ask for advice, and her earlier family traumas may have made her less trusting that others would be helpful. Given her resources and experiences, she may not have seen a way to maintain a professional identity.

We thus still have much to learn about how identities are formed and when they change. Yet, some issues are clear: both inherited resources and identities are associated with who is downwardly mobile and how they fall.

9

What's Next

Americans tend to celebrate upward mobility, bemoan class reproduction, and, up to now, ignore downward mobility.[1] Now we have a way to understand it. Downward mobility is about inequality—that even in the upper-middle class, not all youth are raised with the same resources.

To remain a college-educated professional or to marry a college-educated professional, it helps to grow up with the resources that professional workplaces and professional spouses reward. Both look for candidates with high levels of human capital (academic knowledge and skills) and professional employers look for youth who have the experiences provided by economic capital (money) and cultural capital (knowledge of how to navigate institutions) too.[2] With little of these resources, youth are unlikely to graduate from college and find a professional job or to marry a college-educated professional. In other words, with little of these resources, youth are likely to be downwardly mobile.

The seeds of downward mobility from the upper-middle class then start with the resources youth inherit from their families. Some upper-middle class youth inherit high levels of each resource. Later, they internalize identities that guide them to acquire more resources and maintain their resource strengths. With these inherited and acquired resources, they easily reproduce their class position. Other upper-middle-class youth inherit low levels of at least one resource—at least compared with their peers in their class. Later, they internalize identities that encourage them to forgo opportunities to turn their resource weaknesses into resource strengths. Without a full complement of resource strengths, they struggle to graduate from college, enter the professional workforce, or marry a college-educated professional. Most are downwardly mobile.

The answer to who is most apt to fall from the upper-middle class is then those with inherited resource weaknesses and nonprofessional identities. And the answer to how they fall is by enacting identities that make a virtue of their resource weaknesses or that lead them away from maintaining their resource strengths. Of course, not all downwardly mobile youth foresee their

Privilege Lost. Jessi Streib, Oxford University Press (2020) © Oxford University Press.
DOI: 10.1093/oso/9780190854041.001.0001

slide toward a lower social class. Why would they? Some spend a lifetime observing a parent who is firmly in the upper-middle class and who has the same resources and identity as their own. Others observe that their own re-sources and identities move them closer to class reproduction while they are in school and college. Why would they imagine that professional workplaces would not do the same? Without anticipating downward mobility, they do not change who they are or what they do. They are, after all, becoming the people they long wanted to be.

Unanswered Questions

This study answered questions about who is at risk of downward mobility, how they fall, and why they do not see it coming. Yet, it still leaves some questions unanswered. Who is included in the study's conclusions? What other resources might shape downward mobility from the upper-middle class? And how can the resource-identity model of downward mobility help us understand variation in siblings' mobility trajectories?

To Whom Do the Findings Apply?

The study followed 107 youth as they transitioned to adulthood. All were white, all were born between 1984–1990, and all were born into the upper-middle class. Would the results be the same if we considered downward mo-bility of other groups, born in other times, and from different classes?

The question is unanswerable with the data at hand. However, we can speculate. In all cases, we are likely to see that resources and identities shape mobility trajectories, but the extent to which each matters likely changes by group and time. Thinking about race, it is well known that structural barriers and discrimination make it difficult for black and Hispanic parents to secure and pass on as many resources to their children. Black and Hispanic parents' incomes are usually lower; they are more likely to be excluded from networks and opportunities that provide institutional knowledge; and they are more likely to be unmarried, incarcerated, and, for black parents, to have health problems.[3] Black and Hispanic parents are then likely to have and transfer fewer resources—factors that put their upper-middle-class children at risk of downward mobility through no fault of their own. In addition, the link between inherited resources and identities is likely to vary by race. Identities respond to communities, and research shows that whites are less likely to identify and treat black and Hispanic youth as professionals.[4] Moreover, black and Hispanic youth's inherited and acquired resources are less likely to be tightly connected to class reproduction. They must use their resources in the context of widespread discrimination—making it likely that high levels of resources will not translate into maintaining an upper-middle-class position as often. At each step of the process—inheriting resources, identity formation, and using their acquired resources to avoid downward mobility—black and Hispanic youth are disadvantaged compared to whites in their class.[5]

If we considered downward mobility from another social class, we might also see differences. Again, identities are shaped by communities, and the identities available in each community are likely to differ. Upper-class women may have a socialite identity available to them; working-class men and women may have a worker identity available to them—a person who lives to work but not in a professional job. These identities will also shape what resources youth acquire and what class they enter as adults.

In addition, there may be different connections between inherited resources, identities, acquired resources, and mobility in different time periods. The youth in this study entered the labor market during and around the Great Recession. In this time period, it was mostly youth with inherited resource strengths and professional or family men identities who reproduced their class position through work. In periods with more jobs, we might see more class reproduction for other groups. For example, there might be more professional jobs available to artists and to family men born with resource weaknesses. In a better economy, we might also see more early marriage—potentially allowing more explorers to reproduce their class position through their spouse. And, of course, different time periods will bring different community values, different identities for youth to occupy, and different rates by which members of different identities take up each identity. Resources and identities may always matter for mobility, but they will matter in different ways.

How Do Unstudied and Studied Resources Matter?

Inherited resources are typically the unmoved mover[6] in the story of downward mobility from the upper-middle class.[7] This book focused on three such inherited resources—academic skills, institutional knowledge, and money as measured by household income. However, two additional resources are prime candidates for moving youth's mobility trajectories: non-parental social connections and parental wealth. This book did not focus on social connections because it seemed, surprisingly, less relevant to early mobility trajectories. This is because once respondents' identities were formed,[8] youth with nonprofessional identities tended to ignore or not seek out people who would help them gain resources they did not receive or accept at home.[9] Youth with professional identities sought out and drew upon their connections more—perhaps quickening the path they were on but not changing it. Wealth may have mattered more for youth's trajectories—possibly shaping the identities youth formed or their consequences. However, the data on which this study is based does not include useful measures of wealth. We will need more data to make the connections between wealth, identities, and mobility clear.[10]

We also need to know more about the resources that this study did include—economic, human, and cultural resources. I defined resource strengths and weaknesses as relative to those in their social class, but it is not entirely clear how best to conceptualize resource strengths and weaknesses. Did resource weaknesses relate to identities because youth observed peers with more resources, because institutions have an absolute standard that those with resource weaknesses did not meet, or because of each? If it is the former, would youth who grow up in class-segregated communities develop different identities than youth who grow up in class-integrated ones? Also, when and how do youth develop a sense of their relative resources, do any get it wrong, and if so, what are the sources and consequences of their misperception? And, from a research perspective, where, exactly, should the line be between resource strengths and resource weaknesses?

Finally, for youth in this study, acquiring high levels of economic, human, and cultural resources was nearly synonymous with class reproduction. However, a larger sample would likely reveal more variation. Not all individuals with these resources will find jobs, and not all will do so quickly after graduating from college or graduate school. In these cases, we still need to understand how resources and identities matter for mobility.

How Do Siblings' Mobility Trajectories Diverge?

Not all youth in the same family experience the same mobility trajectory. Thinking about resources and identities help us think about why.

Within some families, children receive different resources. Sometimes this is due to parents believing their sons and daughters need different things, but it also can be due to the timing and degree of parents' work commitments, health issues, obligations to extended family, and the resources that come and go through marriage, divorce, and remarriage.[11] In addition, children in the same family may enter different communities. A family's geographic move, a change in religious affiliations, or children's own perceptions of their community may make different identities more noticeable and alluring. The timing of experiencing these resources and communities will likely matter for identity formation as well, with early resources and communities having an outsized effect. And, of course, youth's other identities and traits—their gender, learning difficulties or abilities, and health, for instance—will shape what resources they receive and what identities they adopt. When they receive different resources or enter different communities, children in the same family are likely to enter different social classes.

The Lies My Country Told Me: Insights About the Class Structure

Americans grow up listening to myths about how people rise and fall in the class structure. The American Dream tells us that we control our class fate, that anyone can work hard and get ahead, and that life in the upper-middle class will provide great freedoms. The ideas we grow up with are simply untrue—even for youth born in the upper-middle class.

The Myth of the Self-Made Man

This book shatters a myth about the American class structure—that of the self-made (wo)man. The youth who remained near the top of the class structure did not do so alone—they were enabled by the resources given to them and the environments that prodded them. Likewise, the downwardly mobile did not fall on their own. The resources they were given and the communities that guided them nudged them in particular directions too. Even upper-middle-class youth then did not chart their own course but were guided by factors beyond their control.

And, it was not only that their mobility pathways were not fully self-made, but youth's identities were not either. Americans tend to think of ourselves as free to define who we are, what we want, and how to obtain it.[12] Yet, we always do so in a context, and different contexts make different identities available and valuable. Most people, it seems, take on the same identity when they are raised in the same circumstances—suggesting that social environments play a powerful role in who we become.

Moreover, youth were not even self-made (wo)men during the transition to adulthood—a life stage that social scientists claim offers profound freedoms for recent upper-middle-class cohorts.[13] Social scientists see the new transition to adulthood as a moment of heightened agency—a time to explore, to follow one's own path, and to become "self-made." Yet, while youth's transitions to adulthood were varied, they were not free. Most youth marched to adulthood in lockstep with those who shared their resource inheritances and identities. They did not explore or claim new freedoms but moved toward to becoming who their resources and communities long positioned them to be.

The Role of Hard Work

There was no rest for the privileged. The most privileged respondents typically became professionals and worked tirelessly in school, college, and professional jobs. Nancy skipped showers to devote herself to academic work, Molly skipped out on friends, and both spent most of their time striving for achievement in these institutions. Not all professionals worked as hard as Nancy and Molly, but in an economy that rewards academic knowledge and institutional insights, many professionals dedicated great time and energy to acquiring the resources they needed to stay in the upper-middle class.

Yet, it would be wrong to say that hard work led to class reproduction or that the lack of it led to downward mobility. Instead, we need to reimagine how hard work matters for social mobility. The public often thinks of hard work as a precursor to a privileged adulthood,[14] but it may be the result of a privileged childhood as well. Those privileged enough for their hard work to pay off usually worked hard. Those disadvantaged enough to sense that their hard work would leave them behind tended to work less hard. Hard work itself was a privilege—it showed that one was born with enough advantages to rationally believe that there was a connection between effort and outcomes.[15]

The Myth of Downward Mobility as a Signal of an Open Class System

Social mobility is often framed as providing evidence of an open class system—where people rise and fall for reasons unrelated to their class of birth.[16] This view is too narrow. The class system may have been somewhat open when considering class origins, but it was far more closed when considering inherited resources. Youth who fell were not individuals who competed on a level playing field and lost, but those who were raised with fewer resources than their peers. Even within the upper-middle class, there was not a meritocracy.

Moreover, who was downwardly mobile signaled that the class system was not open to individuals of all identities either. Stay-at-home mothers, rebels, artists, athletes, and most types of explorers were most likely to fall. With some types of people so much more likely to fall than others, downward mobility again did not signal an equal opportunity system for all.

The Costs of Class Reproduction

We tend to think of class reproduction as a personal good—the privileged are able to stay privileged. But class reproduction was neither all personal nor all good.

There was an impersonal benefactor of class reproduction: professional employers. From an early age, professional youth entered an unwritten contract with them. Youth who identified as professionals researched employers' standards, devoted themselves to meeting them, and internalized employers' goals. In return, employers rewarded them with a job that would keep them in the upper-middle class. As long as they defined a good life as a working life, they could stay ahead.

This unwritten contract offered professionally identified youth class reproduction, but it was packaged with profound costs. All goals and activities that might interfere with becoming a good worker were delayed, downplayed, or disparaged. Professional youth put off dating; their adolescence was a time for honing their workplace skills, not learning about love. Professionals did not experiment with goals or approaches or senses-of-self like explorers did; why would they when they knew they wanted to tie their identities to work? Professionals did not test the limits of their autonomy, break rules for the thrill of it, or engage in purely hedonistic activities like rebels did. To do so would risk their future as a professional worker. Perhaps most importantly, professionals rarely contemplated what their goals should be if they lived for a purpose other than to be a good worker. For professionals, these costs were not burdensome as they internalized employers' interests. But others might find these costs too much—some would gladly trade class reproduction for the ability to pursue other goals.

Methodological Insights My Forbearers Did Not Tell Me

We learn how to study from those who came before us—those whose successes we wish to emulate. But following in our forbearers' footsteps can lead us to travel well-worn paths rather than to also discover new ones.

The Importance of Within-Class Studies

Many of the most popular qualitative studies of social class inequality have a common methodological design: they study differences *between* classes rather than differences *within* classes.[17] These studies have provided important insights about how class works, but they also come at a cost. They have left us with overgeneralized portraits of each class, faulty assumptions about how class works, and little attention to social mobility.

The typical qualitative study of social class compares upper-middle-class and working-class respondents.[18] The analyst then identifies the main approach taken by respondents in each class while telling the reader little about the variation within each group. This has left us with oversimplified ideas of the upper-middle class. Typically, upper-middle-class parents are portrayed as highly resourced, informed, hands-on, and motivated to maintain their children's class position.[19] This may be true of the modal upper-middle-class parent or mother, but it ignores that upper-middle-class parents also vary considerably on each dimension. Yet, without understanding the variation in the upper-middle class's resources and approaches, we will struggle to understand variation in their outcomes.

The between-class approach also produces a faulty assumption: most of what the upper-middle class does is effective at reproducing their class position. This assumption comes from comparing the approaches taken by upper-middle-class families and working-class families, noticing that they are different, and observing that institutions favor the upper-middle-class approach.[20] However, without a within-class comparison, we miss that there are many ways that upper-middle-class families engage with institutions. Not all are rewarded by institutions or effective at keeping upper-middle-class youth in the upper-middle class.

In addition, qualitative between-class approaches tend to focus on respondents in the same communities.[21] A within-class approach allows us to expand past studying one place and to see that conservative communities shape mobility paths in different ways than liberal communities. Whereas youth in liberal communities often reported that their parents were intensely focused on maintaining their academic and institutional knowledge, youth in conservative communities more often said that their parents prioritized other goals—becoming a good family member and religious congregant. To understand mobility, we then cannot only focus on liberal communities located near research universities. We must examine the diversity of upper-middle-class communities too.

The Need to Study Youth's Resources, Not Only Parents' Class Position

If we looked only at Bert's and Joe's parents' class position, it would be hard to tell them apart. Both had two parents with master's degrees and professional jobs, and their parents' earnings were not far apart—with Joe's parents earning slightly more than Bert's. If we define social class by education and occupation, or even education, occupation, and income, we would think that Bert and Joe were raised in the same social class and had the same propensity to fall from it. However, if we looked at the resources they inherited from their parents, it would be clear that they did not have equal chances of falling. Bert's hands-on parents gave him high levels of human and cultural capital, while Joe's parents did not. Clearly, Bert was better poised to avoid downward mobility than Joe. If we want to understand who will enter what class as an adult, we are better off measuring the resources that children inherit from their parents than the class position or resources their parents possess.[22]

The Need to Consider Resources and Culture

Researchers debate the same issues that liberals and conservatives do: whether resources or culture most determines individuals' class positions.[23] Versions of this debate assume that resources and culture are independent from one another—they proceed as if individuals were equally likely to adopt any goals or take any actions regardless of their resources. As this book has shown, it makes little sense to talk of individual goals and practices without talking about inherited resources as well. We should be talking about resources *and* culture rather than resources *or* culture.

What parts of culture should we talk about? Identities and values, among others. Identities provide packages of goals, actions, and ideas of what is valuable—they orient youth toward a particular future and give them ideas of how to achieve it. Community values are also important as they nudge individuals into identities and remind youth what types of people and actions deserve respect. Both are important as they relate to what resources youth seek out—and therefore what mobility path they are likely to take.

To avoid blaming the victim, sociologists have shied away from studying identities and values in the context of social mobility.[24] But individuals are pushed into identities that emphasize particular values by contexts and resources outside of their control. Thus, talking about identities and values does not mean blaming the victim—it means talking about how different contexts shift what values are attainable and what identities are esteemed. Moreover, by not studying values, we implicitly use our own. Researchers frame downward mobility as a negative outcome rather than as a trade-off youth make to pursue goals that they value more.[25] Instead of considering identities and values off-limits when considering class, we would then be better off studying them—further understanding how communities develop and maintain values, how individuals form identities and goals, and how each relates to social mobility.

The Power of Interviews

Interview studies have recently come under sustained critique, with sociologists arguing that people do not do what they say or know why they do what they do.[26] But if we assume that people say what they think, then interview data can help us understand downward mobility.

To understand downward mobility, it is important to know what people think. Some goals are aligned with class reproduction and some are not. Asking people what their goals are is the only way to find out; researchers cannot discern goals from observations. How people frame institutions also relates to their mobility trajectory, and we cannot know how they do so unless we ask. To only observe them would lead researchers astray. Researchers might assume that a teen who identifies as stay-at-home mother is trying her best in school when, in reality, her low grades reflect her other priorities. Researchers might think that an explorer does not know how to navigate college to reproduce her class position. Through interviews, we may learn that she does know but does not always act on her knowledge—she pursues other goals instead. In short, interviews help us separate what people do not know from what they know but choose not to do.[27]

Interviewers also tend to agree with the idea that people do not know why they do what they do—manuals for how to interview respondents warn researchers against asking "why" questions.[28] But while interviewees cannot tell us why they do what they do, interview data can give us strong hints. As shown in this book, the analyst can map the contextual factors of individuals' lives—their resources, communities, and other relevant contexts—onto what they say. The analyst can use respondents' stories to propose theories of why people do what they do—even if unknown to the respondents themselves.

Lessons for Parents

Mobility pathways are not entirely in youth's control, and they are not entirely in parents' control either. Still, there are lessons for parents about how to increase their children's chances of becoming upper-middle-class adults— and why they should not worry about implementing them.

Reframe Downward Mobility

Many upper-middle-class Americans experience profound anxiety about their children's potential downward mobility.[29] Before parenting to avoid downward mobility, parents should consider if doing so is truly in their children's interest. If professional parents are like professional youth, they define success in narrow ways. They see success as emanating from school and workplace achievements more than from family, leisure, or self-growth. They may also downplay the degree to which professionals can be viewed as company's abiding servants—people who surrender much of their lives to meet corporate needs.

Parents, then, can remind themselves that their definitions of success are not the only valid ones and their children's views of success may not correspond to their own. To some, life in the middle and working classes brings its own benefits. It allows youth to focus on family, be independent, practice the arts, live a varied life, and not revolve their worth around their work. And, while downward mobility may come with a loss in status, it does not mean that youth who experience it are disadvantaged overall. Resource weaknesses, after all, means resource weaknesses compared with youth born in the same social class. And, while life in the lower classes may be less economically secure, their children will still be better off than the vast majority of the world's children.[30] Before parenting to avoid downward mobility, then, parents should consider if the costs of downward mobility are as high as they believe, if the costs of class reproduction are as low as they assume, and if their children's goals—even ones that lead away from class reproduction— might be worth pursuing.

Invest Early and Continually in Children's Resources

If parents still want to help their children avoid downward mobility, the main lesson of this study is simple: they need to provide their children with high levels of human, cultural, and economic resources from an early age. In other words, having a high income alone is unlikely to be enough to prevent children's downward mobility—parents need to pass down academic and institutional knowledge too.

Providing children with high levels of resources is not an easy task— even for families who have them. Transferring resources requires large time investments. Moreover, transferring the "right" resources challenges arrangements common to conservative families. These families tend to have the parent with the least academic and institutional knowledge in charge of parenting; children are then raised by parents who would not be in the upper-middle class on their own. It would be easier for upper-middle-class children to stay in the upper-middle class if they were raised by parents with the resources consistent with that class. In many families, this means fathers will need to play a larger role in raising their children or nonprofessional mothers will need to spend more time understanding how the professional labor force works.

Identity Formation and Maintenance

Parents whose primary goal is for their child to remain in the upper-middle class should make sure that their child knows that they value a professional identity. This means that parents should talk often of the rewards work brings, highlight professionals' achievements, and push children to focus more on work than marriage. Parents of children who have already developed nonprofessional identities have two options for pushing their children toward a class reproduction track. They can give them the resources that would encourage them to change identities or encourage them to acquire these resources themselves. The latter is most likely to work when parents give advice aligned with their children's identities. The parents of women who identify as stay-at-home mothers can tell their daughters that divorce rates are much lower for women with college degrees than women without them. The parents of family men can tell their sons that a greater focus on school and work will increase the likelihood that they become a stable provider. Artists can be pointed to professional jobs that reward their talents and also have an air of economic disinterest—they can use their artistic skills to become a marketer for non-profits or the arts. Rebels can be pointed to jobs that allow them great autonomy, such as professional sales jobs or entrepreneurship. Explorers can be taught about professional jobs that allow them to combine their interests—jobs that allow more flexibility, autonomy, and change. The point is to align advice with youth's identities.

Help Children Identify Generational and Life Course Change

It is difficult for children to anticipate downward mobility given generational and life course change. Their experiences are limited, and they may not know what lays ahead. Parents can learn about these processes and help their children understand them. Exposing their children to people who have experienced generational or life course change may be useful in alerting their children to where their pathway will lead.

Lessons for Policymakers and Voters

It is often said that many voters do not begrudge the rich—they want to be them.[31] In the same spirit, upper-middle-class voters should not to begrudge the middle class, working class, or poor—they or their children may become them. Voters should then support policymakers who will ensure an easier life for everyone—one with better schools, health care, jobs, and wages.

This point is vital. For anyone who read this book worried about their own or their children's potential downward mobility, it is important to remember that the life conditions of the working class and poor relate to public policies. Health, safety, and economic opportunities need not correlate with class to the extent that they do. We can lessen apprehension of downward mobility by making life in the working class easier for all, and we can all do our part by electing politicians who support pro-working-class platforms.

If we cannot make life easier for everyone, we can at least change the rhetoric around social mobility. We can recognize that being born with the most resources is the clearest path to remaining at the top of the class structure. We can acknowledge that people work hard toward varied goals and that motivation toward work can be a luxury of the privileged. We can agree that if those who are born at the top have to do so much to stay ahead, it will be remarkably difficult for those born with less to rise up the class ladder. At the very least, we can avoid blaming and shaming the downwardly mobile. Instead, we can help those born with and who end up with less.

Moving Forward

We leave Julie, Vera, and the 105 other youth soon after they became adults. As they grow older, many will maintain their identities and the mobility pathways that follow. Others will come to understand the implications of generational and life course change and try to jump tracks. Still others may discover new identities that become available as they age.[32] And some will change trajectories due neither to inherited resources or identities, but to health problems, divorce, layoffs, and economic changes.

Of course, if their futures are like their older peers, the majority will remain on the mobility trajectories they started down long ago.[33] The power of their pasts is strong—with their early resources and communities shaping who they are, what they want, and what mobility path they are most likely to remain upon.

Data and Methods

Analyzing the Lives of American Youth

This book develops a new model of downward mobility by studying the lives of young Americans who participated in the National Study of Youth and Religion (NSYR).[1] Despite its name—the National Study of Youth and *Religion*—this data set has features that allow for a new understanding of social mobility. Normally, qualitative researchers follow youth for short periods of time and then speculate about how the findings shape respondents' class position years later.[2] These studies also tend to stop at the college gates, giving the false impression that college graduates will necessarily avoid downward mobility. The NSYR data set has no such limitations. It follows a large sample of youth for nearly half of their lives—10 years—from high school until after they graduate from, opt out of, or return to college. Moreover, whereas qualitative studies are often limited to youth who live in a particular geographic region,[3] the NSYR not only includes youth in commonly studied states like New York, Massachusetts, and California but also includes youth in less visited places, like Idaho, Utah, and Alabama. Finally, the NSYR data set is immune from suspicion that interviewers steered youth's comments to generate a particular finding about downward mobility. Rather, interviewers were focused on religion, not mobility, making it unlikely that they even unconsciously shaped respondents' answers in this way. This data set—unconventional for studies of social mobility—then is perhaps one of the best for generating insights about it.[4]

This appendix reveals more about the lives of the youth selected for the NSYR—how they ended up in the study, who they are, what they were asked, and how I drew upon their stories to study downward mobility.

Making Calls: Collecting Data for the NSYR

In 2002, a team of researchers set out to talk to American youth. Wanting to understand a cross-section of American teens, they called American households using a random-digit dialer—a technique that comes close to ensuring that every qualified US resident had an equal chance to participate in the study. The researchers told those who answered the phone that they were conducting the "National Youth Study" to learn about the lives of adolescents. If there were no 13 to 17 year olds in the house, they politely thanked the speaker for their time and continued making calls until they reached households with teens. They then asked a parent about their child's life and asked to talk to the teen about their own life. When there was more than one teen in the house, they used a systematic method of choosing who to talk to: the teen whose birthday had most recently passed. As youth agreed to tell their stories, the National Study of Youth and Religion (NSYR) was born.

In all, the NSYR team surveyed 3,370 youth—a sample that they confirmed was representative of the American population of 13-to-17-year-olds more broadly.[5] These surveys provided an overview of the lives of youth born between 1984 and 1990—a cohort often viewed as among the most privileged upper-middle-class children in American history.[6] Yet, the researchers wanted to learn more—to hear from youth in their own words. So, from their sample of 3,370 youth, they chose 267 teens to talk to in more detail. They chose the interviewees in a strategic way; they used a stratified quota sample to find even numbers of respondents based on their geographic region, location (urban, rural, or suburban), age, gender, race, household income, religion, and school type. They also wanted to learn more about groups that are typically under-represented in social science research, so they oversampled three groups: youth who were homeschooled, attended private school, and were Jewish.[7]

The NSYR team then took a rare and important step: they followed respondents for over a decade, interviewing them from their teens into their 20s. They conducted four separate waves of interviews, catching up with respondents every two to three years. The team also learned so much from the interviews that they decided to add more respondents to the study; in waves three and four they invited more survey respondents to be interviewed. They chose new respondents using the same criteria as in earlier waves: they filled quotas by geographic region, location (urban, rural, or suburban), age, gender, race, household income, religion, and school type.

Making Cuts: Refining the Sample

The NSYR team interviewed youth born into all social classes. Since this book focuses on youth who were born near the top of the class ladder, I limited the sample to the 107 white youth who began their lives in the upper-middle class and who completed a fourth-round interview. Just as Americans do not agree on what counts as upper-middle class, sociologists do not either. In fact, sociologists do not agree on the criteria that should be used to define classes in general, how many classes there are, or where the line between one class and another falls. Since there is no standard way to define the upper-middle class, I used parents' education and occupation. These criteria are relevant to many theoretical approaches of social class, are commonly used by class scholars, and correspond to how many Americans think about class.[8] I included every interview respondent who had at least one parent who was both college-educated and a professional at wave 1, when respondents were 13 to 18 years old. I defined college educated as having completed a bachelor's degree or more. I used the US Department of Labor's data set, the O*NET, to define professional jobs. The O*NET classifies every job and assigns it to a job zone. Job zones are ranked 1 through 5 based on the education, experience, and training needed to do the job. I defined professional jobs as those in Job Zone 4 and Job Zone 5—the jobs that employ workers with the most education, experience, and preparation. These jobs include teachers, accountants, and loan officers at the lower end and CEOs, judges, and psychiatrists at the upper end. In addition, I included small-business owners and graduate school students as professionals.

I also focus the book on a single racial group: whites. I used an inclusive definition of white—anyone who had at least one white parent. Though this definition counters the traditional way that Americans think about race, it makes sense in this context. Many of the youth with one white parent were coded as white by at least one of their interviewers, implying that they have the skin tone that comes with advantages. Moreover, having one white parent gives youth access to some of the resources that comes with their race—resources like wealth and social connections. I focus only on whites for theoretical and methodological reasons. Theoretically, their downward mobility is the most difficult to explain as it cannot be explained by racial discrimination. Methodologically, the NSYR contains too few upper-middle-class respondents of a single nonwhite race to meaningfully understand their mobility pathways.

Making Data: Interviewing Respondents

The NSYR team conducted the 300-plus interviews that form the basis of *Privilege Lost*. The team consisted of a sociology professor, Christian Smith, and several of his colleagues and graduate students. Each interviewer was trained to ask for respondents' and parents' consent, to choose a public place to conduct the interview that was out of the earshot of respondents' family members and friends, to conduct the interview, and to handle unusual situations. The team then dispersed across the country, meeting youth near their homes. Interviewers often spoke to respondents who shared their race and gender, and, when possible, the same interviewer talked to the same respondent in each wave of the study. Interviews varied in length, but generally lasted around two hours.

Each trained interviewer followed a structured interview guide. This ensured that every respondent heard the same questions, no matter who asked them. The interview guide covered several of the same topics across each wave, such as respondents' relationships with their parents and their ideas and experiences concerning school, work, romantic relationships, organized activities, and religion. In most interviews, respondents also had space to talk about any other important events happening in their lives.[9]

At the end of the interview, the interviewer took steps to allow others to understand the respondent's life. The interviewer first turned the audio recording of the interview over to the NSYR team, who in turn made sure that each interview was anonymized, transcribed, and archived.[10] In addition to turning in the audio files, the interviewers recorded notes about the people they interviewed. They wrote about what the respondent looked like, what clothes they wore, and their demeanor. I did not interview any respondents myself, so when I refer to a respondent's appearance, I am referring to interviewers' descriptions of the respondents.

Making Sense of the Sample

As youth ended the study, they began their lives as adults. This moment marked the beginning of their class position being defined by their own education and occupation and the end of it being solely determined by their parents. At an average age of 26, about half of the upper-middle-class NSYR interview sample—53%—were on class reproduction trajectories, while the other 47% were on downwardly mobile trajectories. Among the downwardly mobile group, just over half had graduated from college but not obtained a professional job, while just under half had neither graduated from college nor received a professional job.

How does the interview sample compare with the national population? I used the Panel Study of Income Dynamics (PSID) to answer this question as the interview data included few respondents chosen in a non-random manner and the NSYR survey collected little data on nonresidential parents. Among white youth born between 1984 and 1990, about half were downwardly mobile around age 26—they had not received a college degree and professional job or married someone who did. The proportion of the interview sample who was on a downwardly mobile trajectory was then consistent with the nationally representative sample.

Of course, readers may question whether respondents really fell. Are young adults downwardly mobile if they were unemployed but lived in their parents' home? Were they downwardly mobile if they had a college degree they could use one day but hadn't yet? Were they downwardly mobile if their parents had wealth that could cushion their fall? This book considers young adults in these situations to be on downwardly mobile trajectories. Although they may have the comforts of an upper-middle-class life and the possibility of re-entering the upper-middle class, they had not yet secured a place in the upper-middle class themselves. Moreover, most youth who are downwardly mobile at age 26 remain downwardly mobile at age 40.[11] These early stages of adulthood usually portend what is to come.

Readers might also wonder if extreme privilege is disguised as downward mobility. Perhaps some children do not need to attend college or find a professional job to stay ahead. While this is undoubtedly true for families with great wealth, it is not true for the typical upper-middle-class child. Parents' wealth helps children graduate from college and purchase a home, but it rarely helps them leave the labor force.[12] When upper-middle-class parents are living, they transfer about $70,000 to their children from the time when they are 18 to 34 years old—not enough to live on comfortably for many years.[13] And, after upper-middle-class parents pass away, most leave their children with an inheritance the size of a few years of an upper-middle-class young adult's annual income.[14] Not surprisingly, then, no respondent in the sample said that they would never need to work or to marry someone who did.[15] Downward mobility would result from not finishing college and finding a professional job or not marrying a college-educated professional.

Other readers may wonder if defining mobility by education and occupation understates the amount of downward mobility. The child of a financial manager who becomes a teacher, for instance, would reproduce her class position but earn far less than her parent. This is true, and income certainly matters for young adults' opportunities. But pointing to teachers as people who are paid little shows that our vision of the class structure is skewed. The average salary for a teacher is $56,383[16]—a figure far above $31,099,[17] the median income for one American, and closer to the median *household* income, a figure that often includes a second earner.[18] Teachers are then still at the upper end of the American class structure, even by income. They are also among the top one-third of Americans in terms of education. Some may still believe that the child of a financial manager who becomes a teacher is downwardly mobile, but considering the big picture, they do not fall very far.

Finally, some may think that the real measure of downward mobility is subjective— if people feel worse off than their parents. The problem with this approach is that perceptions are often very far from reality. Some people in the top 1% of the income and wealth distributions truly feel middle class and some feel downwardly mobile.[19] Some professional parents worry that they need to accumulate tens of millions of dollars to prevent their children from falling.[20] Though these individuals' perceptions are sincere, taking them too seriously obfuscates the true amount of inequality in this country.

Making Sense of Downward Mobility: Analyzing the Data

With the above definition of downward mobility in mind, I took an abductive approach to analyzing the data. The abductive process takes an agnostic stance toward analyzing data.

The analyst may extend existing theories, though not ones that have been selected before-hand, or may develop an original theory.[21]

The analytical process itself is akin to putting together a jigsaw puzzle. The analyst takes cues from how others have assembled puzzles but, in regard to one's own puzzle, does not initially know what counts as a puzzle piece, how each piece will fit with others, or what the end picture will be. Along the way, the analyst frequently restarts after she realizes the puzzle pieces she identified will not add up to a whole and regularly disassembles pieces she later realized she jammed together. To determine the puzzle pieces—the important factors and processes associated with downward mobility—and how they fit together, I read each transcript multiple times, created over 300 codes, used spreadsheets to doc-ument who said and had what when, drafted dozens of memos, created piles of charts, checked emerging analyses against the data, and revised analytical insights after receiving feedback from others. Below I describe where each primary puzzle piece comes from and how I defined it.

Different aspects of the argument—different puzzle pieces—come from different sources of data. Information on parents' income comes from the parent survey, which was administered when respondents were 13 to 17 years old. Parents marked which in-come bracket reflected their household earnings. They were given options in $10,000 increments, beginning at $0 to $10,000 and ending at $100,000 or more. I report median household incomes. All medians were under $100,000.

Data on parents' education and occupations comes from both the parent survey and the youth interviews. When information from the parent survey and the youth interviews conflicted, I used youths' identifications of their parents' educations and occupations. Youth's perceptions were important as they act upon what they think they know.

I used the interview data to classify whether respondents had at least one hands-on college-educated professional parent. I considered parents to be hands-on if the re-spondent described talking to them frequently about school, college, or professional work. When respondents described their parents differently over time, I noted this as a resource change. In the tables, I privileged the interviews that took place when the re-spondent was age 18 or younger. It is important to note that the classification of hands-on and hands-off is from the youth's perspective, not their parents' perspective.

I defined resource strengths and weaknesses using parents' incomes, educations, occupations, and youth's reports of hands-on parenting. In terms of economic capital, I defined youth as having a resource weakness if their household income was $70,000 or less, or if their parents refused to pay for their college education or co-sign a student loan. I defined a resource strength as households earning more than $70,000 annually. In this sample, a household income of $70,000 put youth near the lowest third of the sample's income distribution, potentially making it noticeable to respondents that they had access to fewer economic resources than others in their social class. Resource weaknesses and strengths related to human and cultural capital were defined by whether the respondent had at least one college-educated professional parent who was also hands-on. Strengths referred to having such a parent and weaknesses referred to not having one.[22] Of course, there is a spectrum within hands-on and hands-off parenting, and, as the explorers' chapter reveals, I made judgement calls on just how hands-off some parents were. I counted youth who described rarely seeing or talking to their parents as the most hands-off, and youth who regularly talked to their parents about subjects other than school, col-lege, and professional work as less hands-off.

I also classified each respondent as coming from a liberal or conservative commu-nity. Research shows that liberal and conservative family types map onto geography and religion.[23] I used both as cues. I defined liberal communities as ones located on the East Coast from Maryland north, communities on the West Coast, and left-leaning cities and suburbs in other places in the country—cities like Atlanta, Austin, Chicago, and Minneapolis. I defined conservative communities as all others. I also counted anyone who was a member of a conservative religion as living in a conservative community—regardless of where they lived—and used the Pew Foundation's information to classify denominations as conservative or not.[24]

My classification of youth's identities comes from the interview data. Identities reflect goals and approaches to school, college, work, and marriage. I coded the interviews for these themes. Usually goals and approaches aligned; in the rare cases when they did not, I classified respondents by their goals.[25] Goals and approaches corresponded with identities in as shown in Table A.1.

As the table shows, identities corresponded to particular distinctions. Professionals, family men, artists, and athletes might each want professional jobs; what differentiated them was the type of work they wanted and the role they wanted work to play in their lives. Family men emphasized marriage and fatherhood more than work, and artists and athletes wanted to enter winner-takes-all labor markets—ones in which only the very best performers receive stable jobs.[26] In this way, an artistically inclined person who wanted to become a graphic designer would be a professional while an artistically inclined person who wanted to sell her own paintings would be an artist.

As I determined each youth's identity, I also needed to figure out how many identities appeared in the data. I used three guiding principles to define the number of identities: (1) I determined identities inductively, in accordance with respondents' goals and approaches to school, college, work, and marriage; (2) I categorized respondents in the least number of identities that made sense in the data; and (3) I collapsed categories when discussing them separately would not lead to any new analytical insights. Thus, while others may have paid more attention to the internal diversity within each identity—for example, that professionals included people who strove to become social workers, doctors, and engineers—I did not as their resources, approaches, and mobility pathways were similar.

The Assumptions Embedded in This Book

The goal of this book is to draw on the life stories of over 100 youth to build a new theoretical model of whites' downward mobility from the upper-middle class. As in any study, the data do not reveal all we want to know, and so I rely on several assumptions to build my argument. I outline them here.

- The respondents in this sample are not a random sample of the population, but I assume that they are also not unique. The factors that lead to their mobility trajectories are likely to lead to the same mobility trajectories for others like them—even if not to the same extent.
- I assume that respondents' descriptions of their inherited resources are more-or-less accurate, or that their perceptions matter more than the reality. I also assume that the amount of human and cultural capital parents possess is highly correlated with their education and occupation.
- I only "meet" respondents at age 13, at the earliest, and I assume that the resources and communities they describe are similar to those they accessed earlier or are as they described having when they were younger.

Table A.1 Classification of Identities

Primary Goal	Example of Goal	Primary Approaches	Identity
Professional job	"I want to go into law or forensic science."	Devoted to academics and professional work	Professional
Stay-at-home mom	"Hopefully, I'll be able to get married and have a family, and I will be a stay-at-home mom."	Displays emotional distance from academics and work; devoted to romantic relationships	Stay-at-Home Mom
Marriage, fatherhood, and providing	"My highest life priorities are finishing school and getting in a career that's going to provide for my family."	Displays emotional distance from academics and work; devoted to romantic relationships	Family Man
No career or family goals*	"[I have] no concrete goals I'm really going after."	Shows sustained opposition to school, college, work, and marriage	Rebel
Winner-takes-all arts or sports job	"I'm interested in filmmaking."	Devoted to a winner-takes all pursuit	Artist or Athlete
Multiple	"I still picture myself as being a stay-at-home mom" and, for the same respondent in the same interview, "It's hard for me to imagine not working."	Combines multiple of the above, without a single allegiance to any	Explorer

* A few rebels do have career goals: they want a working-class job. I do not count this in the definition as these respondents tended to be in the upper-middle class by a technicality more than in practice.

- By the time I "meet" respondents, their identities are already formed. I assume that their resource environments and communities came before their identities. I make this assumption because I see parallels between identities and a habitus—a mental structure that stems from early childhood environments.[27] It is also not the case that respondents' descriptions of their parents simply match their own identities. If this was the case, they would describe each of their parents in the same way—a practice that often did not happen.

The reader can decide how likely it is that my assumptions are true, and I hope future researchers investigate them further. For now, what the book offers is a new theoretical framework—one that can move us closer to understanding which upper-middle-class youth fall, how, and why so many of them do not see it coming.

Tables

This appendix contains four tables that support the claims made in this book. All tables refer to data from the 107 white upper-middle-class respondents in the National Study of Youth and Religion (NSYR). Table A.2 shows the inherited resources and mobility trajectories of respondents. Table A.3 shows how identities relate to youth's resources and communities. Table A.4 depicts the book's theoretical model, including what percent of respondents with each identity were downwardly mobile. Table A.5 supports the claims made in chapter 8. Among youth with similar inherited resources, identities relate to mobility pathways; among youth with similar identities, resources relate to mobility trajectories.

Table A.2 shows that respondents on downwardly mobile and class reproduction trajectories tended to have different sets of inherited resources. Respondents on downwardly mobile tracks tended to have lower family incomes and less often had at least one hands-on, college-educated professional parent. The table also shows that what differentiated the two groups was less their parents' educations and occupations than whether they had a *hands-on*, college-educated professional parent.

Table A.3 shows how inherited resources and communities relate to identities. For example, the first column shows that professionals tended to have relatively high incomes, at least one hands-on, college-educated professional parent, no serious health issues or learning disabilities, and grew up in liberal communities—secular ones near the coasts or in left-leaning cities. In contrast, the second column shows that women who identified as stay-at-home mothers tended to grow up in families with high incomes, without a hands-on, college-educated professional parent, and in conservative communities—either in conservative religions or in the heartland of the country. Subsequent columns show the resources and communities related to each identity.

Table A.4 shows that resources and communities map onto identities and that each map onto mobility trajectories. In the sample, the least likely youth to be on downwardly mobile trajectories are those with resource strengths and professional identities. All other groups had a larger percentage of members on downwardly mobile pathways.

Table A.5 shows that among youth with similar resources, identities relate to mobility. Among youth with resource strengths, a higher proportion of youth with nonprofessional identities were on downwardly mobile trajectories than youth with professional identities. Among youth with resource weaknesses, the same pattern held.

Similarly, among youth with the same identity, resources related to downward mobility. Within each row—each identity—a larger portion of youth were downwardly mobile when they had resource weaknesses than when they had resource strengths.

Of course, these numbers are quite small and come from a non-random sample. However, they are aligned with the idea that both resources and identities relate to downward mobility.

Table A.2 Inherited Resources and Mobility Trajectories of Respondents

	Downward Mobility Trajectory	Class Reproduction
N	50	57
Inherited Resources Related to Economic Capital		
Parents' Median Household Income[1]	$75,000	$95,000
Inherited Resources Related to Human and Cultural Capital		
Percent Mother With BA or Higher[2]	72	84
Percent Father With BA or Higher[2]	100	86
Percent Both Parents With BA or Higher[2]	69	68
Percent Stay-at-Home Mother Without a BA	12	7
Father's Job Zone[3]	3.58	4.15
Father's Job Zone[3]	4.24	4.25
Percent Hands-Off Mother	46	21
Percent Hands-Off Father	76	34
Summary: Inherited Resources Related to Human and Cultural Capital		
Percent With at Least One Hands-On College-Educated Professional Parent	30	79
Percent With Learning Disability or Health Issue Preventing Transmission or Use of Human and Cultural Capital	14	3

Source: Data is from the interview part of the National Study of Youth and Religion. Interviewees are white and have at least one college-educated professional parent. The mean age of respondents in both class reproduction and downward mobility pathways is 26 years old.

[1] Parents' median household income is measured through the NSYR parent survey, administered when respondents were 13 to 17 years old. The survey used close-ended questions asking parents which $10,000 increment captured their household income. I set these increments at their midpoints (e.g., an income of $90,000–$100,000 was $95,000). Incomes were recorded in 2002–2003. They are not adjusted for inflation.

[2] Percentages show the number of mothers or fathers in the category divided by the number of mothers or fathers in the category for whom the parents' educational attainment is known. Unknown parental education usually reflects that the parent does not live with the child. I am missing father's educational information for five respondents who were downwardly mobile and six respondents who reproduced their class position. BA = bachelor's degree.

[3] O*NET classifies jobs into five zones based on the amount of education, training, and experience required. Jobs in Zone 5 usually require a graduate degree. Jobs in Zone 4 typically require a BA. Jobs in Zone 3 or lower do not typically require a BA. Stay-at-home and unemployed parents are excluded from job zone averages. *Source*: US Department of Labor, O*NET (https://www.onetonline.org).

Table A.3 The Correspondence Between Identities, Inherited Resources, and Communities

	Professional	Stay-at-Home Mother	Family Man	Rebel	Artist & Athlete	Explorer	Total/Avg.
N	40	10	14	11	10	22	107
Inherited Resources Related to Economic Capital							
Parents' Median Income[1] (in 1000s of dollars)	95	95	80	85	45	75	85
Inherited Resources Related to Human and Cultural Capital							
Percent Without at Least One Hands-On College-Educated Professional Parent	20	90	50	82	30	55	45
Percent with Learning Disability or Health Issue Preventing Transmission or Use of Human and Cultural Capital[2]	5	10	21	0	10	9	8
Summary: Percent Without a Hands-On College-Educated Parent or With Health Issue Preventing Transmission or Use of Human and Cultural Capital[3]	23	100	50	82	40	55	48
Community							
Percent Conservative Religion	18	60	64	0	30	27	29
Percent Heartland[4]	23	70	79	27	10	41	37
Summary: Percent Conservative Religion or Heartland[2]	33	80	93	27	40	50	49
Demographics							
Percent Women	58	100	0	9	30	64	48

[1] Parents' median household income measured through the parent survey, administered when respondents were 13 to 17 years old. Survey used close-ended questions asking parents which $10,000 increment captured household income. I set these increments at their midpoints (e.g., an income of $90,000–$100,000 was $95,000). Incomes recorded 2002–2003 and not adjusted for inflation.

[2] Health issues were self-reported. Issues included cancer, depression and anxiety that led to missing days of school, attention deficit disorder, and unspecified issues leading to placement in special education classes. (Issues are probably undercounted; not all youth with learning and health issues are likely to report them.)

[3] Summary measures are not equal to the sum of the two measures as each respondent can occupy both categories.

[4] Heartland is operationalized as noncoastal non-liberal communities.

Source: Data from the interview part of the National Study of Youth and Religion. Interviewees had at least one college-educated professional parent. The mean age of respondents in all identity groups is 26 years old.

Table A.4 Theoretical Model: How Inherited Resources, Communities, and Identities Relate to Downward Mobility

Inherited Resource Weakness	Community	Identity	Primary Mobility Pathway	Percent Downward Mobility	N
None	Liberal	Professional	Class Reproduction	13	40
Human & Cultural Capital	Conservative	Stay-at-Home Mother	Downward Mobility	70	10
None or Human & Cultural Capital	Conservative	Family Man	Both	36	14
Human & Cultural Capital	Liberal	Rebel	Downward Mobility	82	11
Economic Capital	Either	Artist or Athlete	Downward Mobility	90	10
None or Any	Either or Both	Explorer	Downward Mobility	68	22

Note: Proportion downwardly mobile comes from the interview part of the National Study of Youth and Religion. Because the interview sample is not nationally representative, the numbers should be read as an indicator of a pattern rather than as generalizable. A small number of respondents changed identities; they are included in the category with their earlier identity.

Table A.5 Inherited Resources, Identities, and Downward Mobility

	No Resource Weaknesses			At Least One Resource Weakness		
	N	Number Downwardly Mobile	Percent Downwardly Mobile	N	Number Downwardly Mobile	Percent Downwardly Mobile
Professional	27	1	4	13	4	31
Stay-at-Home Mother	0	0	0	10	7	70
Family Man	4	1	25	10	4	40
Rebel	2	1	50	9	8	89
Artist/Athlete	2	1	50	8	8	100
Explorer	6	3	50	16	12	75
All	41	7	17	66	43	65

Note: Resource weaknesses refer to inherited, not acquired, weaknesses. Inherited resource weaknesses include low levels of human, cultural, or economic capital compared with others in the sample. Low levels of human and cultural capital is operationalized as not having a hands-on, college-educated, professional parent. Low levels of economic capital is operationalized as $70,000/year or less per household or having parents who refuse to pay for college or co-sign student loans. Respondents who changed identities are included in the category with their earliest identity.

Source: Data from the 107 upper-middle-class respondents in the interview part of the National Study of Youth and Religion.

APPENDIX 3

Theory

Revising Bourdieu

Anyone who knows Pierre Bourdieu's work will notice that this book draws from it. At first blush, this may be surprising as the primary critique of Bourdieu's work is that it explains class reproduction without explaining social mobility.[1] While not using all of Bourdieu's notoriously complex terminology, this book has extended his ideas to account for downward mobility. This appendix describes how.

The French sociologist Pierre Bourdieu composed one of the most well-known theories of class reproduction.[2] In Bourdieu's model, there are different segments of each social class, each defined by the capital that they possess. Individuals raised in each segment of each class internalize a habitus—a set of goals, strategies, worldviews, and tastes—from the direct and indirect socialization they receive in their childhood class position. The habitus is durable and transposable, encouraging individuals to act in patterned ways across time and institutional domain. In each time and place, individuals are geared to want what they have, make a virtue of what they lack, and feel comfortable where they are. The habitus then tethers individuals to their class origin by guiding them to navigate their social environment[3] in ways that will keep them in it.[4] As shown in Table A.6, the habitus works similarly to identities, with the exception that the latter is more conscious and is organized around a public archetype of a person.[5]

Bourdieu's version of the habitus helps explain class reproduction but not downward mobility. If everyone in the same segment of a social class has the same habitus, then, barring a sudden change in the class system,[6] they should reproduce their class position. To understand variation in the class trajectories of individuals born in the same social class, we need to modify one aspect of his theory of the habitus: the habitus is not formed through *class socialization* but through a related but distinct concept: *resource inheritances.*[7]

To Bourdieu, the habitus is formed through class socialization. In this model, individuals raised in the same social class—or the same segment of the same social class—are exposed to the same cultural milieu and material reality. Specifically, class position is defined by the father's occupation,[8] and children raised in the same segment of the same social class receive the same direct and indirect socialization from the family, the school, and the broader community. They then develop a set of goals, strategies, and worldviews that match the environment in which they were raised. There is nearly a one-to-one correspondence with the class of their childhood and the habitus they internalize, or what one researcher calls "ontological complicity between habitus and habitat."[9] As such, nearly everyone in the same social class develops the same habitus. The habitus orients people to reproduce their class position, and with the same habitus, nearly everyone in the same childhood social class becomes adults in the same social class.[10]

Table A.6 Habitus and Identity

	Habitus	Identity
Developed in Childhood	X	X
Durable over Time	X	X
Transposable across Settings	X	X
Provides a Sense of People Like Me	X	X
Varies by Field	X	X
Makes a Virtue of Necessity	X	X
Reproduces Itself	X	X
Conscious		X
Maps onto a Public Archetype		X

However, if the habitus does not come from *class socialization* but from *resource inheritances*, then we can understand how downward mobility occurs. For a child to gain resources, the family members with the resources typical of their class must actively pass them down and children must accept them—passive socialization will not do. Fathers are also not necessarily more influential than mothers—what matters is who has the resources typical of their class and who passes them down. Not all family members have resources typical of people in their social class, those that have them do not all actively pass them down, and children are not always able to accept them. The variation in family members' resources and transference processes creates space for children raised in families in the same social class to inherit different resources. Youth then develop a sense of how their inherited resources compare to those around them. They develop a habitus based upon their own relative resource strengths and weaknesses[11]—not their or their father's class position—and their habitus provides the goals and strategies that reproduce their resource set.[12]

Figure A.1 illustrates the differences between the class socialization and resource inheritance models of the habitus. In the figure, H refers to human capital, C to cultural capital, and E to economic capital. Pluses refer to a large amount of the resource relative to people in their social class and minuses refer to a small amount of the resource compared to people in their class. Arrows represent active resource transfers, and thick dark lines indicate that the transfer was not accepted. The figure focuses on a subset of upper-middle-class families and simplifies them, presenting only cases when at least one parent has high levels of all three forms of capital.

Box 1 shows Bourdieu's class socialization model. In this model, the family is a unit defined by the father. The family passes down its resources to their children. In Bourdieu's model, this occurs because children pick up what they need to know not only from direct socialization but, importantly, also from indirect socialization that occurs simply by growing up in a classed environment. By growing up in the same class as their fathers, children acquire the same resources and reproduce their class position.[13]

Boxes 2–6 show non-exhaustive examples of this book's resource inheritance model—one that does not abide by the class socialization model's premises of indirect socialization and father-centered families. As the illustrations in these boxes show, fathers' resources do

CLASS
SOCIALIZATION

RESOURCE
INHERITANCE

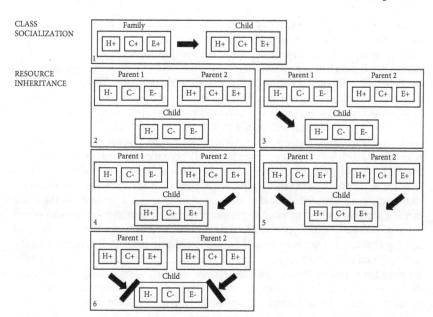

Figure A.1 Class Socialization and Resource Inheritance Models Among the Upper-Middle Class

Note: The figure presents a non-exhaustive image of resource inheritance models. Parents are presented as having low or high levels of all resources compared with their class. In reality, each parent may have high levels of some resources but not others.

not define the family's resources—it is necessary to examine the resources that each parent holds. In the upper-middle class, one parent may have high levels of resources, as shown in boxes 2, 3, and 4, or both parents may have high levels of resources, as shown in boxes 5 and 6. In addition, families vary in the degree to which they actively pass down their resources. Transference processes include but are not limited to that no parent actively passes down resources (box 2), the parent with few resources for their class passes them down (box 3), the parent with many resources for their class passes them down (box 4), both parents with high levels of resources pass them down (box 5), and parents pass their resources down but children do not accept them (box 6). When neither parent actively transfers their resources (box 2), the parent with low levels of resources for their social class is the main transmitter of family resources (box 3), or children do not accept their parents' resources (box 6), children will inherit few resources relative to others in their social class.[14] When one (box 4) or two (box 5) parents with high resources transfer them to their children, their children will inherit more resources. In this way, upper-middle-class youth will inherit different resources depending on their family transference processes. They will also develop different habitus, with children raised in the systems depicted in box 2, 3, and 6 internalizing different habitus than the children raised in the systems depicted in box 4 and 5. Once their habitus is formed, it will orient them to reproduce their *resources*, not their class position.

Of course, it is not the habitus itself that determines mobility patterns, but the interaction between the habitus and institutions. Institutions reward individuals who have a habitus that matches their expectations; institutions make it difficult for individuals with other habitus to advance through them. Bourdieu maintained that upper-middle-class youth typically have the habitus that upper-middle-class institutions reward.[15] To him, mismatches between upper-middle-class youth's habitus and the one that institutions reward only occur when a structural change suddenly erupts or after youth are already socially mobile.[16] However, a resource inheritance model of the habitus suggests otherwise. Mismatches between upper-middle-class youth's habitus and the institutions that facilitate class reproduction will occur with regularity and prior to social mobility. Mismatches will occur when no parent transfers their resources to their child, when the parent with few resources for their social class serves as the child's primary socialization agent, or when the child does not accept their parents' resources.[17] Some upper-middle-class youth with resource weaknesses and the habitus that follows will then be rejected by upper-middle-class institutions. More will opt out of the institutions that would not celebrate them and define a different path as superior to the one that would be difficult for them to take.[18] Among youth born in the upper-middle class, those who inherit resource weaknesses and develop a habitus that makes a virtue of them are among the most likely to be downwardly mobile. Those who inherit resource strengths and develop a habitus that maintains them are poised to remain in their original social class. In short, a single change—positioning the habitus as formed by and oriented toward reproducing resources[19] rather than class position—can account for both class reproduction and downward mobility.[20]

The resource inheritance model of the habitus also raises the possibility of understanding the precursors to upward mobility. Youth raised in the working class will not receive or internalize a uniform set of resources. Some parents will have and pass down more resources than others, and some children will be better positioned to acquire their parents' resources than others.[21] Some youth will also find non-parental sources from whom to gain resources—potentially extended family members and mentors. Those who receive high levels of resources compared to other working-class youth are especially likely to develop a professional habitus—one that leads them to seek out more resources.[22] To the extent that they are able to acquire more resources in their communities and that no unsurmountable crises occur, they may be upwardly mobile. Those who are raised with resource weaknesses, even relative to those in their class origin, will instead be likely to maintain their class position.[23]

To study upward and downward mobility we will then need to design studies that match the resource inheritance model of the habitus. Doing so means replacing studies that measure class position with studies that measure the resources available to each child. If we cannot measure resource inheritances directly, we might be able to measure the habitus directly. Though the habitus is notoriously difficult to operationalize and measure,[24] the fact that it maps onto identities gives us ways to study it.[25] Researchers can inductively map the identities available to people in each demographic group in each social class then use surveys to ask a wider range of respondents which identity or identities best describe them. The combination of these new theoretical understandings and methodological approaches will allow us to extend Bourdieu's work to understand social mobility as well as class reproduction.[26]

Acknowledgments

Writing this book has been the most difficult professional project I have conducted. The abductive process is always difficult, and it is even more difficult with the benefits of a large data set. Reading and analyzing over 300 interviews to understand how downward mobility occurs has been an enormous challenge.

I have many people to thank for getting me here. I thank Sasha Killewald, Tova Walsh, and Steve Vaisey for conversations that led to this book. This project also only took off after I presented a theoretical article in the Duke culture workshop about the role culture plays in social mobility. That day, Steve Vaisey told me about the National Study of Youth and Religion and suggested I look into it, and Lauren Valentino and Nick Bloom stayed after the workshop to convince me to look into the data and pursue this project. I likely would not have written this book—at least not now and not in this way—had I not presented in the workshop that day. I thank Lauren for inviting me and Steve, Lauren, Nick, and the other workshop participants for their encouragement to pursue the project.

Once I started working on the project, many people helped along the way. I thank Sara Skiles, the NSYR data administrator, for helping me access the data and answering my questions. Lauren Valentino provided me lists from the survey data with respondents' parents' occupations, educations, and incomes. Two Duke undergraduates, Emily Cohen and Erik Savereide, helped with the final round of coding. Marcus Mann, a Duke graduate student at the time, used the NSYR survey data to provide background information about the amount of mobility among young adults and who experiences it. Michael Burrows, a Duke public policy graduate student, used the Panel Study of Income Dynamics to analyze the association between being downwardly mobile as a young adult and a middle-aged adult.

Several people read and commented on drafts of the book. I owe a special thank you to Mark Chaves who read two entirely different versions of the book, went over the initial reviews with me, and provided incredibly useful feedback. Nick Carnes and Jack Metzgar also read a full version of the book and provided invaluable feedback. Sasha Killewald, Shamus Khan, David

Swartz, Steve Vaisey, and Lauren Valentino were gracious enough to attend a book workshop where they offered such insightful feedback that it convinced me to rewrite the book from scratch. Several others also read individual chapters or the book proposal or commented on earlier versions of this project through a talk. These include Chris Bail, Carolyn Barnes, Callie Cleckner, Joanne Golann, David Harding, Allison Hurst, Ellen Lamont, Haiyi Liu, Lisa Keister, Betsy Leondar Wright, Abigail Ocobock, Rick Rodems, Josipa Roksa, Martin Ruef, Michael Schwalbe, Jacklyn Wong, the Yale Center for Research on Inequalities and the Life Course, the University of Maryland Population Research Center, and the University of North Carolina Culture and Politics workshop. I also thank the reviewers who pushed me in the right direction, and my editor, James Cook, who has patiently seen this book through.

Many people have also provided support throughout the process. I always tell job candidates that I can't imagine any other department rivals Duke in the time they allow their assistant professors for research, and I thank the department for allowing me the time to work on this book. In addition, while I was writing the book, Linda Burton, Linda George, and Lynn Smith-Lovin served as mentors, and I am grateful for their support. When I arrived at Duke, I also asked for advice about being an assistant professor, and one of my colleagues told me to rely on my graduate school training. I am forever grateful for my time at the University of Michigan—for the professors and graduate students who made the department such an enriching and welcoming community.

It's also hard not to write this book and reflect on my own advantages. I thank my parents for providing me with the resources to reproduce my class position and for their tolerance of the downsides of a professional identity—working too much. Their resources also keep coming—my mother was the first to read a draft of the whole book. I also owe a big thank you to my partner, Rob, who serves as a sounding board, offers statistical advice, and puts up with my endless frustration about how much inequality exists in the world.

And, finally, I thank the respondents who I have never met, but whom graciously volunteered to tell interviewers about their lives and to let other researchers analyze them. I also thank Christian Smith and the NSYR team for collecting their stories and making them available to other sociologists. Of course, this book would not have been possible without them.

Notes

Chapter 1

1. All names are pseudonyms.
2. I thank Michael Burrows for generating this number. It comes from an analysis of the Panel Study of Income Dynamics. The analysis is based on youth born from 1984 to 1990 who had at least one college-educated professional parent during that period.
3. There is no consensus about how to define the upper-middle class, but sociologists commonly use education and occupation in their definition (Lareau and Conley 2008).
4. As respondents were born in the 1980s but also lived with their parents in the 1990s, I include trends over both decades when making this statement.
5. Autor (2014).
6. Putnam (2015).
7. Altintas (2016); Kornrich and Furstenberg (2013).
8. Bloome (2015); Reeves (2017); *The Economist* (2015); Thompson (2014).
9. Schwartz and Mare (2005).
10. Banta (2015); Kearney and Levine (2015); Reeves (2017); Streib (2017); *The Economist* (2015); Thompson (2014).
11. Altintas (2016); Hays (1996); Kornrich and Furstenberg (2013); Lareau (2011).
12. From here forward, unless otherwise stated, when I refer to upper-middle-class youth, I mean upper-middle-class *white* youth.
13. Beller and Hout (2006).
14. The downside of measuring social mobility by education and occupation is that it defines away upward mobility from the upper-middle class. Upper-middle-class youth have a highly educated parent at the top of the occupational structure; there is little room for them to achieve more. For this reason, Sherman (2017) argues that we need to use income and wealth to understand upward mobility. As the respondents in this book are only followed through their mid-20s, income and wealth cannot help us understand intergenerational mobility. As such, this book only examines class reproduction and downward mobility from the upper-middle class.
15. Sociologists generally prefer to study mobility as an outcome rather than a trajectory and to measure respondents' mobility when they are approximately 40 years old (Torche 2011). Doing so is not possible with the data at hand. Moreover, it may not be overly necessary. Authors who suggest waiting until individuals are 40 years old measure mobility by income—a factor that is far more volatile than education, and, to some degree, occupation, and that changes more with age. By contrast, once individuals have a four-year college degree, they always have one, and many upper-middle-class youth receive these degrees by age 22 (Zarifa et al. 2018).

16. Torche (2011).

17. The average age of respondents in the sample is 26.

18. I thank Michael Burrows for this analysis. Numbers come from an analysis of the Panel Study of Income Dynamics (PSID). The analysis refers to the 1,272 white households in which the respondent was born into the upper-middle class and was between 38 and 42 years old in 2011, 2013, or 2015. Due to the PSID's data limitations, the analysis does not include youth who did not form their own household by age 26. The PSID also has higher attrition rates for youth born into the upper-middle class who are downwardly mobile than youth born into the upper-middle class who reproduced their class position (Schoeni and Wiemers 2015). These data limitations should be considered when evaluating the percentage of people who are downwardly mobile at age 26 who stay downwardly mobile around age 40.

19. Beller and Hout (2006); Ferrare (2016); Hout (2019).

20. Ferrare (2016), figure 2, refers to 25-to-65-year-olds.

21. Beller and Hout (1996). Their numbers refer to men born between 1950 and 1979. Hertel and Groh-Samberg (2014) found similar rates of occupational downward mobility among men born between 1972 and 1979. Studying an extended time period, Hertel (2017) found more occupational downward mobility among daughters of professionals than among sons of professionals—suggesting it may be less than one in two children of professionals who remain professionals. There may be more downward mobility now than in the past. Hout (2019:29) found: "Millennials might be the first American generation to experience as much downward mobility as upward mobility, though they are still young enough to make up lost ground. Among Americans born in the late 1980s, 44 percent were in jobs with higher socioeconomic status than their parents, and 49 percent were in jobs with lower socioeconomic status than their parents." However, Hout's (2019) numbers refer to all Americans, not just those with professional parents. Also note that Chetty et al.'s (2018) widely-read study about downward mobility examines income rather than occupation and education.

22. Analysis comes from Michael Burrows's analysis of the PSID. The number is based on whites only, and youth born between 1984 and 1990 who had at least one college-educated professional parent in that time. In this analysis, downward mobility is measured at age 26.

23. Of course, to understand how many upper-middle-class youth are likely to be downwardly mobile, we not only need to know how many slots are available in colleges, the professional workforce, and as spouses to college-educated professionals but also how much competition there is to obtain these spots. This is shaped by birth and death rates, immigration, and competition from youth born in other social classes.

24. Karabel (2005).

25. Alon (2009); Kahlenberg (2010); Pérez-Peña (2014); Santoli (2002); Stevens (2009).

26. Hoxby (2009).

27. See Houle (2014) on debt; see Astin and Oseguera (2004) on the increase of children with college-educated parents who attend college. Of course, the availability of student debt was not the only reason upper-middle-class students' college attendance increased.

28. Grusky, Western, and Wimer (2011).
29. Horowitz (2018); Posselt and Grodsky (2017); Vaisey (2006); Wodtke (2015).
30. Abel, Deitz, and Su (2014).
31. Mare (2015).
32. Cherlin (2010).
33. By some accounts, these contextual factors decreased upper-middle-class youth's odds of class reproduction, while by other accounts they increased it. Measuring social mobility by occupation, Mitnik, Cumberworth, and Grusky (2015) found that class reproduction among the upper-middle class increased for the cohort studied in this book compared with past cohorts. However, measuring intergenerational mobility by income—which is correlated with, though different than, occupation-education mobility, Mathur and Kallen (2017) found that the children of upper-middle-class parents fell particularly far during this period. I have not seen a published trend analysis of how likely upper-middle-class youth are to not become a college-educated professional or to marry one.
34. We currently know little about who falls and how. The last major book on downward mobility was Katherine Newman's (1988) *Falling from Grace*—a book that came out around the time when Julie and Vera were born. It also looked at intragenerational downward mobility rather than intergenerational downward mobility.
35. The interviews were interpreted through the lens of Bourdieu's theory of how class works. In particular, I rely on his theory to make connections that the data suggest but cannot prove. His theory suggests that individuals' resources come *before* their identities. The data I used for this study begins when respondents are 13 to 18 years old and have already formed identities—making it impossible to know that resources predate identities. For this claim, I rely both on respondents' accounts of their earlier childhoods (ones that, of course, might be influenced by their current identities), and, more heavily, on Bourdieu's claim that identities (or what he would call a habitus or a sense of "people like us") follow from resources.
36. Based on an analysis of the PSID.
37. Many other explanations of downward mobility fit into this model as they relate to the resources children inherit or the identities they display. For example, parents' health relates to the resources youth receive, and children's drug use displays a rebel identity. Of course, some explanations of downward mobility will not be captured by this model, such as when an adult child is downwardly mobile after leaving work to take care of a loved one—despite having the resources and identity that enable her to stay in the upper-middle class.
38. Bourdieu (1986) introduced these capitals. Importantly, Bourdieu also defined cultural capital as including the tastes of the dominant classes. I limit my definition of cultural capital to knowledge about how to navigate institutions. Arguably, knowledge of how to navigate institutions is more important than elite tastes for avoiding downward mobility. Youth must pass through school, college, and professional work if they are to remain in the upper-middle class on their own, but they do not need to have elite tastes to do so.
39. Social capital is usually included along with these resources. However, for teenagers, social capital can help them gain human, cultural, and economic capital but is likely

to be less important on its own. To the degree that it mattered, it seemed to be in changing youth's identities. Artists, in particular, pointed to teachers as generating their interest in the arts.

40. Bourdieu (1980, 1984, 1986).

41. Bailey and Dynarski (2011); Murnane and Reardon (2018); Rivera (2015); Stevens (2009).

42. Bourdieu and Passeron (1977); Kusserow (2004); Lareau (2011).

43. Mare (2015).

44. Parents' economic capital also includes their wealth. Unfortunately, I do not have access to data on parents' wealth. Therefore, I do not include it here.

45. Mare (2015); Schwartz and Mare (2005).

46. Of course, parents with the same amount of money can have different ideas of how much to give their children (Lacy 2007). I do not know the amount of money parents spent on their children, but I take into account one aspect of their spending. I count respondents as possessing low economic resources for their class if their household income was less than $70,000 a year or if respondents said that their parents did not pay for college or co-sign student loans. The latter only occurred in rare cases.

47. Lahire (2011).

48. Alm (2011); Bloome (2017); Conley (2005); McLanahan and Sandefur (1994); Streib (2015).

49. I focus on whether youth were *able* to accept and use the resources their parents provided rather than if they were *willing* to do so. Being unwilling to follow parents' advice about school, college, and work could reflect an already-formed identity. Rejecting parents' advice outright can show a rebel identity; quietly ignoring it may reflect that youth have prioritized family (the stay-at-home mother or family man identity) or leisure activities (the artist and athlete identities) and see little need to focus on school and professional work. Instead, I focus on learning disabilities, physical health, and mental health issues that make it difficult for youth to internalize or use their parents' advice. In the tables and text, I only include issues that youth mention. Of course, some respondents likely have undiagnosed or undisclosed conditions as well. Taking them into account would reduce the number of youth categorized as exceptions.

Parental warmth also relates to whether children accept their parents' resources (Taylor, Clayton, and Rowley 2004). Many parents who lack warmth are also hands-off—and are therefore captured in the model. Others are not captured for the same reason as above. If a child calls his parents cold, I cannot tell if the child is displaying an already formed identity (a rebel) or became a rebel because their parents' lack of warmth made it difficult to accept his parents' resources. Future research with more longitudinal data should discern which comes first.

50. It seems straightforward that upper-middle-class youth with more resources will avoid downward mobility more often than upper-middle-class youth with fewer resources. However, this has not been thoroughly documented. Qualitative studies of social class portray nearly all upper-middle-class youth as having high levels of economic, human, and cultural capital and as reproducing their class position (for

example, Calarco 2018; Lareau 2011; Stuber 2011). Ignoring both variation within upper-middle-class youth's resources and variation in their mobility pathways, they have yet to examine whether the two are related. Quantitative studies often compare children's class position to their parents' class position or children's income to their parents' income, but neither approach captures the confluence of resources— economic, human, and cultural—that children and parents possess. Moreover, the few quantitative studies of mobility that do examine the upper-middle-class's varied resources tend to focus on parents' resources rather than the resources youth receive from their parents (see, for example, Alm 2011 and Thijssen and Wolbers 2016). The two are not the same, and it is the resources youth receive from their parents, not their parents' resources themselves, that is most likely to explain who remains in the upper-middle class and who falls.

51. Sociologists define identities in many different ways. I recognize that my definition is different than many.

52. The ideas of rejecting what has not been offered and making a virtue of necessity come from Bourdieu (1984).

53. And, of course, gender relates to identities too. Clearly, women are more likely to identify as stay-at-home mothers and men are more likely to identify as family men.

54. Cahn and Carbone (2011).

55. Cahn and Carbone (2011).

56. See Keister and Sherkat (2014) for more on the relationship between religious communities and social mobility.

57. Note that if we measured parents' resources rather than children's access to their parents' resources, we would see different patterns. Parents' earnings would still vary, but all children would have at least one college-educated professional parent. We would then not be able to observe one of the most important associations between resources and mobility: youth who receive little human and cultural capital from their parents are likely to be downwardly mobile.

58. For example, students can strategize about how to receive scholarships to attend college. Public universities often offer "merit" scholarships—ones that disproportionately go to white students from upper-middle class backgrounds (Heller and Marin 2002).

59. The phrases "inherited" and "acquired" come from Bourdieu (1984).

60. Cahn and Carbone (2011).

61. Coontz (2016).

62. Fortin (2005).

63. Coontz (2016).

64. Parents tend to have relatively stable incomes and occupational categories (professional or not). Upper-middle class white families are among the least likely to experience income volatility (Pew Research Center 2017).

65. In this way, I intend identities to be akin to the habitus (Bourdieu 1984). Of course, others argue that identities constantly change. Giddens (1991) and Illouz (2008) are some of the lead voices in this regard. However, while they effectively argue that identity change is encouraged in popular culture and that people talk of trying to change

their identities, they do not show how often identities actually change. Moreover, the types of identities they refer to are not those related to archetypes but those related to micro-characteristics. In the model put forth in this book, identities reflect resources and communities. As long as these do not change, we would not expect identities to change often either.

66. Here I don't mean that respondents necessarily thought about their class position explicitly. But many people do think of their ability to enact particular lifestyles, and those lifestyles are loosely connected to a class position.

67. Of course, upper-middle-class youth remain in the upper-middle class at higher rates than we'd expect by chance.

68. Hout and Janus (2011).

69. Beller and Hout (2006); Hout and Janus (2011).

70. And, it is worth remembering that even the poorest Americans are richer than the majority of people in the world. As *New York Times* writer Catherine Rampell states when discussing Branko Milanovic's work: "The typical person in the bottom 5 percent of the American income distribution is still richer than 68 percent of the world's inhabitants."

Chapter 2

1. I do not name the communities to protect respondents' anonymity and to abide by the National Study of Youth and Religion (NSYR) data-use agreement.

2. Molly grew up with the assumption of having a liberal family form. However, it is unclear whether she grew up as a member of a conservative religion. She identified as Christian but did not associate with a denomination. If she was a member of a conservative denomination, it did not shape her ideas of family life. Instead, she put her religion in service of her professional identity: she prayed for good grades and a good job. She later converted to a different form of Christianity when she thought it would help her advance at work.

3. For example, in the television show *Suits,* the main characters think of their job as their passions, put off weddings to attend to their jobs, and see work as interesting and fun.

4. Jacobs and Gerson (2004) found that professionals work longer hours than nonprofessionals.

5. Blair-Loy (2003); Streib (2015).

6. Currid-Halkett (2017); Hart and Risley (1995); Hays (1996); Walkerdine, Lucey, and Melody (2001).

7. Buchmann, Condron, and Roscigno (2010); Heiman (2015); Lareau (2011); Lareau, Weininger, and Cox (2018).

8. Metzgar (2019).

9. Grodsky and Riegle-Crumb (2010); Mullen (2010).

10. Lamont (2020).

11. Armstrong and Hamilton (2013); Cahn and Carbone (2011).

12. Calarco (2018); Kusserow (2004); Lareau (2011).

13. Bourdieu and Passeron (1977); Calarco (2018); Kusserow (2004); Rivera (2015).
14. Blair-Loy (2003).
15. Bowles and Gintis (1976) wrote that this is how class reproduction among the upper-middle class works. Class reproduction happens as people align their own interests with the interests of their workplaces.
16. Nancy saw achievement in school as directly connected to becoming a professional. She expressed as much when, at age 18, she compared herself to her friends:

> I feel very different from almost all of my friends. It has partly to do with ambition, because I have a lot of ambition in my life. There's things I want to do. There's things I want to accomplish and I want to get done. A lot of my friends are very laid back. Like I got my honor's diploma and I had to work very hard for that. And they're like, 'It doesn't help you, why would you do it? Leave it alone, just if you skate by, that's all you need to do.' Like almost every single [State] high school student, almost all of them will attend either [State University 1 or State University 2], and they are just planning on getting all their basic requirements for their basic degree, doing their basic job, getting a basic, just a very basic life, which is fine for being content and everything. But I know that I would never be content if I didn't try to go and do something big, you know? I'm always rushing around trying to get things done and I always have something going and I'm always slightly stressed out, which is when I work the best.

17. Nancy, Molly, and Bert also each participated in extracurricular activities. It was not that they did nothing but study, but that academic achievement was their priority.
18. Not all youth who identified as professionals delayed committed relationships. Some used three other strategies to make sure that dating did not interfere with their professional identities: distance, dump, and dominate. In the distance scenario, youth undertook long-distance relationships so that their partners would not interfere with their education or careers. In the dump strategy, youth dated, sometimes quite seriously, but picked their careers over their partners if they conflicted. Arthur, for example, described why he ended his relationship with his college girlfriend, whom he loved: "I don't think either of us wanted to break up, but it just would have hurt more [to stay together]. Because I was like, 'I'm dead-set. I really wanna go small-town rural. I wanna come back here, somewhere in [my hometown region], and practice medicine.' And she's got a strong desire, because she's been overseas on mission trips before, she really wants to go somewhere, like India or Africa. We can't reconcile these two future plans. So that was hard because we didn't want to break up, but we didn't see how it was gonna work out in the long run." Finally, some used the strategy of dominating—telling their partners that they would date them on the condition that their own career came first. For example, Graham told his girlfriend that his career would shape their lives: "I think [work] really affects my life, especially the girlfriend situation. It's like, 'Look, I'm going to medical school for four years and then I'm going to a residency. If my first choice is to be at [East Coast City University] for residency and the computer matches me up in Podunk, Nebraska, I'm moving to Nebraska cause my dream is to be a doctor, I'm going to do it no matter what' . . . We started dating and it was, 'Look, this is what I'm doing.' "

19. Bert was a member of a conservative religion for a short period of time. This may relate to his idea of being less careerist as an adult.

Chapter 3

1. Virginia's family moved frequently. Virginia only mentioned living in predominately rural red states.
2. Rebecca also said her dad went easy on her about school. Her mom did more to monitor her grades.
3. Rebecca's mother was a dancer before being a stay-at-home mother. It is not clear at what level she performed, but even if at a high level, this would make her more of an artist than a professional.
4. Rose (2015).
5. Goldin (1988).
6. The Pregnancy Discrimination Act of 1978, available at https://www.eeoc.gov/laws/statutes/pregnancy.cfm.
7. Charlton (1973); Cherlin (2010).
8. Furstenberg (2008).
9. Rose (2015).
10. England (2010).
11. Fortin (2005).
12. Coontz (2013).
13. Coontz (2013).
14. Crittenden (2010).
15. Coontz (2013); Edgell (2006); Rice and Coates (1995).
16. Stone (2007).
17. Edgell (2006).
18. Gallagher (2004); Gallagher and Smith (1999).
19. Gallagher (2004).
20. Bartkowski and Shah (2014); Uecker and Stokes (2008).
21. Parker and Livingston (2017).
22. Studies find an association between mothers' occupational complexity and children's academic abilities (Kalmijn 1994; Parcel and Menaghan 1994), and find that mothers' employment is positively related to their daughters' employment, occupational prestige, and wages (McGinn, Castro, and Lingo 2019). Studies also find that fathers' involvement in children's lives relates to their children's increased academic abilities (Flouri and Buchanan 2004).
23. Sherkat (2000).
24. Avishai (2008); Edgell (2006); Pearce and Thornton (2007).
25. When Sarah discussed what she talked about with her parents, she defined it by relationships. She talked with her mother about romantic relationships but not with her father.

26. Quotes come from The Church of Jesus Christ of Latter-Day Saints' *Eternal Marriage Student Manual.*
27. Rebecca added that she did not want to get married as early as her peers, but she still thought southern culture played a role in her decision to identify with marriage and motherhood.
28. Of course, there were exceptions. Two women who identified as stay-at-home mothers saw school as about academics. These women wanted short-term careers before becoming stay-at-home mothers.
29. Using the same data set, Uecker and Pearce (2017) also found that women from conservative Protestant religions do not see college as a route to a career.
30. Sarah thought of herself as marrying late but recognized that marrying in her early 20s was still earlier than most Americans.
31. Virginia also struggled to navigate work. She went to beauty school and later regretted it. She wished she had obtained an associate's degree in business—a degree that she thought would offer her more flexibility.
32. Rose (2015).
33. Autor (2014).
34. Waite and Nielsen (2001).
35. Buss et al. (2001).
36. Mare (2015).
37. Mare (2015).
38. Guilder (1986), refers to the percent of women in full-time jobs in 1984.
39. Buss et al. (2001); Mare (2015).
40. Shapiro (2018).

Chapter 4

1. Furstenberg (2008).
2. Coltrane (1997).
3. Coontz (1997).
4. Cherlin (2010).
5. Cherlin (2010).
6. Parker and Livingston (2017); Sayer, Bianchi, and Robinson (2004).
7. Coe (2013).
8. Marini and Mooney (2006).
9. Carlson (1996).
10. Roscigno, Tomaskovic-Devey, and Crowley (2006).
11. Gallagher and Smith (1999); Gallagher (2004). A 2015 *Christian Today* article by Mark Woods quotes Pope Francis as expressing the same sentiment: "Ambition and careerism are incompatible with Christian discipleship."
12. Den Hartog (1985).
13. Dobson, "A Father's Role."

14. *Eternal Marriage Student Manual*: https://www.lds.org/bc/content/shared/content/english/pdf/language-materials/35311_eng.pdf.
15. *Eternal Marriage Student Manual*, p. 74.
16. *Eternal Marriage Student Manual*, p. 202.
17. *Eternal Marriage Student Manual*, p. 207.
18. *Eternal Marriage Student Manual*, p. 201.
19. Mahoney et al. (2003).
20. Bartkowski and Ellison (1995); Dobson (2007).
21. Unlike other family men, Simon described being devoted to academic work and achievement when he was younger. He purposefully decided to put less effort into academics because they made him anxious. His anxiety may have resulted from striving for higher levels of success than his acquired resources made easy.
22. It is not clear exactly what his learning disability entailed. He was in special education courses.
23. To preserve Simon's anonymity, I removed the name of his job.
24. In this quote, Terrence named what type of benefit analysis he does. I cut it to preserve his anonymity.
25. He also talked of having substantial student loan debt and a low credit score.
26. Bastedo and Jaquette (2011).
27. Horowitz (2018); Vaisey (2006).
28. Autor (2014); Bourdieu (1984).
29. Cha (2010).

Chapter 5

1. Depending on one's viewpoint, Colin's rebel identity could be associated with his resources or mismatched with them. He said his parents fought often when he was young—possibly leading him to receive few human and cultural resources as a child. Reading his transcript, it is also hard not to wonder if he has mental health issues, and he suggests his father does. It is therefore my best guess that he either did not receive or could not accept his mother's resource transfers early on. However, it is possible he did and could—and that his identity mismatches his resources.
2. See Evans and Davies (2000) for more on how children's books portray rebels.
3. Kimmel (2008); Schrock and Schwalbe (2009).
4. Coltrane and Adams (1997); Kimmel (2008).
5. Schrock and Schwalbe (2009).
6. Karabel (2005).
7. Flanagan (2014).
8. Armstrong and Hamilton (2013); Sperber (2001).
9. Sperber (2001).
10. Arum and Roksa (2010); Clark and Trow (1966); Sperber (2001).
11. In the quote, Daniel mentions the type of food he serves. I changed the quote to protect his anonymity.

Chapter 6

1. Bourdieu (1983).
2. Bourdieu (1983).
3. Bourdieu (1983); Fontenault (2010); Messineo (2016).
4. There are 10 artists and athletes in the sample. With such a small number, I am again partly relying on past work and theory to make claims about the resource profiles consistent with artists and athletes (see, for example, Bourdieu 1983).
5. Artists and athletes were especially likely to say they developed their artistic and athletic talents and knowledge from sources outside of their parents. They named their teachers as particularly influential.
6. Bourdieu and Passeron (1977); Chambliss (1989); Stephens-Davidowitz (2014).
7. Another possibility is that artists come from families with high levels of wealth but low incomes. They may then be able to appear economically disinterested and still make ends meet. Based on how they describe their families, this possibility seems likely for a few but not for the majority of artists in the sample.
8. In fact, one respondent said that her conservative religion pushed women into the arts. The arts were viewed as a suitable field for mothers as they could focus on their children and produce art on the side.
9. Frank and Cook (1996).
10. Lingo and Tepper (2013); Menger (1999).
11. Eikhof and Warhurst (2013); Wing-Fai, Gill, and Randle (2015).
12. Eikhof and Warhurst (2013); Wing-Fai, Gill, and Randle (2015).
13. Eikhof and Warhurst (2013).
14. Levey-Friedman (2013).
15. Bettie (2003).
16. Karabel (2005).
17. Bowen, Kurzweil, and Tobin (2005); Stevens (2009).

Chapter 7

1. Readers may note that there is no family woman identity. Bell (2013) also finds that young women tend to feel that they need to either focus on work or motherhood and do not see evenly balancing the two as a viable option. It is possible that young women feel that they need to prioritize one more than the other, but as they age a new identity will open up: the working mom.
2. Reba also described her parents as former rebels.
3. Rhonda's difficulty pursuing graduate school and marriage simultaneously parallels family men's difficulty balancing school and relationships. Though a family man is a singular identity, it involves pursuing multiple pursuits (worker and husband) simultaneously.
4. Users of toolkit theory make an odd assumption: because cultural elements are fragmented and used in contradictory ways, they cannot drive action (Swidler 1986,

2003). Explorers' stories show the fallacy of this idea. Explorers held contradictory goals and strategies—each of which mapped onto their actions. They simply followed different goals and used different strategies at different times.

Moreover, some toolkit theorists assume that because cultural elements may be fragmented and used in contradictory ways, they are not patterned or deeply internalized (Swidler 2003). Yet, Bourdieu's (2000b) idea of the divided habitus suggests otherwise. Individuals with a divided habitus regularly hold contradictory goals and strategies and feel torn about what to do. They feel this way because they internalize the expectations of social environments with competing cultural messages (Bourdieu 2000b; Lahire 2011; Sayer 2005).

5. For example, Western New England University (http://www1.wne.edu/arts-and-sciences/mission-statement.cfm) includes in its mission statement a goal of creating well-rounded students: "These complementary abilities, which will provide the foundation for life-long learning and mature decision making, are cultivated in order to help shape our students into well-rounded individuals." The University of Alabama's mission statement focuses on the same: "The University of Alabama is committed to undergraduate education that produces socially-conscious, ethical and well-rounded leaders" (see https://www.ua.edu/about/mission).

6. Blair-Loy (2003); Gerstel and Sarkisian (2006).

7. Other women like Rhonda—women raised with relatively high levels of human and cultural capital in conservative communities—felt that once they figured out who they wanted to be they could become that person. Their husbands' jobs required fewer moves and their own professional interests did not require that they attend graduate school. They continually saw becoming a professional as open to them.

Chapter 8

1. For the sake of simplicity, I divide professional identities from all others. Of course, for youth with resource strengths, the family man identity, and, to a lesser extent, the stay-at-home mother identity, also regularly led to class reproduction.

2. Vana named what type of lab she wanted to enter. I deleted this to preserve her anonymity.

3. Vana was depressed and overweight—factors she also attributed to her dating difficulties. However, women who identified as stay-at-home mothers who were depressed and overweight did marry young. Her mental health and weight were unlikely to be the only issues that affected her marital status.

4. In college, Kendra also distanced herself from people who cared about money. At age 22, she said: "I really dislike these type-As. They're literally just using the [university] name to get out of here and become successful and basically their basis for success is capital, is money . . . There's also a scene at [my college] that I feel is very image-obsessed, very material, obsessed with material goods and wealth. I mean, I like some of those people, but there's a whole scene that literally disgusts me."

5. Respondents with professional approaches that they directed toward working-class jobs were only interviewed in waves 3 and 4 or only wave 4. It is possible that having more information on their earlier lives would change their classification.

6. Or, more accurately, Luke identified as a professional as he grew up but intended to become a family man when he had children.

7. Refers to the 2000 US income distribution, when $81,960 marked the 80th percentile of American household incomes (US Bureau of the Census 2001).

8. Although Luke's father had not graduated from college, he seemed to have high levels of human and cultural capital.

Chapter 9

1. Hochschild (1995).

2. Bourdieu (1980, 1984); Oppenheimer (1988); Rivera (2015).

3. Beasley (2011); Raley, Sweeney, and Wondra (2015); Thomas (1993); Wilderman and Western (2010); Williams (1999).

4. Ispa-Landa (2013); Rios (2009). It is also possible that the model minority stereotype pushes Asian American students into professional identities even when they do not have high levels of inherited resources.

5. That said, there were 24 nonwhite upper-middle-class respondents in the NSYR sample (6 black, 5 Hispanic, 6 Asian, and 7 who held a different racial identity). Among them, there were similar patterns to whites in regard to how identities mapped onto resources, how identities maintained youth's early resource strengths and weaknesses, and how their resources and identities related to their mobility pathways.

6. I take the phrase "unmoved mover" from Swidler (1986).

7. Most youth did not describe major changes in having a hands-on, college-educated professional parent, nor did many describe their families as gaining or losing a major income source. Often, when youth described a change, it was from having a resource weakness to having an even greater resource weakness.

8. At times, respondents attributed their identities to their connections. For example, Max credited his elementary music teacher with introducing him to technical theater. These attributions, however, may be only partially correct. With a different set of resources, they may not have found their connections as influential.

9. The NSYR interview guide asked youth if there were any important adults in their lives outside of their parents and what role they played. Respondents rarely said that other adults gave them information on school, college, or work that they did not also receive from their parents and school. The interview guide also asked respondents about their peers. Most seemed to befriend people who were similar to them, not people who would push them onto a different mobility path.

10. The NSYR parent survey asked parents: "Given the current state of the economy, people are finding themselves in different financial situations. All things considered, would you say that currently your family is in debt, just breaking even, do you

have SOME savings and assets, or do you have A LOT of savings and assets?" This question does not ask parents to provide enough detail about their debts and assets to understand how wealth may shape the class trajectories of youth born in the upper-middle class.

11. Conley (2005); Lundberg (2005).
12. Bellah et al. (2007).
13. Furstenberg (2008); Settersten and Ray (2010).
14. Hochschild (1995).
15. Laurin and Engstrom (2020) make a similar point in regard to motivation for upward mobility.
16. Hochschild (1995).
17. For example, see Armstrong and Hamilton (2013); Bettie (2003); Lareau (2011); Willis (1977). Bloome, Muller, and Schrage (2015:1) also noted: "Typical research practice entails analyzing between-group differences while mentioning within-group variation only in passing."
18. These studies usually refer to the middle class, but actually study the upper-middle class. See, for example, Calarco (2018) and Lareau (2011).
19. Armstrong and Hamilton (2013); Calarco (2018); Cooper (2014); Hamilton (2016); Lareau (2003).
20. This approach comes from Bourdieu and Passeron's (1977) idea that privileged families have approaches that match those that schools expect and reward while working-class families do not. It is repeated in recent studies, most prominently in Calarco (2018) and Lareau (1989, 2011).
21. For example, Calarco (2018); Lareau (2011); Stuber (2011).
22. Of course, this line of question leads to another: What is the right measure of class? If we consider their parents' educations and occupations, and even their incomes, Bert and Joe clearly grew up in the same social class. However, if we think of the resources each inherited, we might draw different conclusions. I would argue that they both grew up in the same social class, as human and cultural capital are measures of resources that tend to correlate with social class but are not measures of social class itself.
23. Small, Harding, and Lamont (2010); Wilson (2009).
24. Or, at least they say they have. See Vaisey (2010) for how sociologists study values without naming them.
25. Of course, it is hard to avoid the idea of downward mobility as only a loss when only examining class position—as opposed to examining many outcomes or what trade-offs youth are willing to make. The language of class—upper, middle, and lower, up and down—also makes it difficult to sound neutral.
26. Jerolmack and Khan (2014); Vaisey (2009).
27. To put it in terms of toolkit theory, sociologists have focused more on what tools people have than why people with the same tools use different ones. To put it in terms of cultural capital theory, stratification scholars are more focused on the capital individuals have than the ends they want to put it toward.
28. Miles, Huberman, and Saldaña (2014).

29. Cooper (2014); Ehrenreich (1989).
30. Rampell (2011).
31. See McCall (2013) on how the reality is more complicated than this popular idea suggests.
32. Women, for example, may take on the identity of the working mom—the woman who tries to balance a job she cares about with the family she cares for and about. For former professionals, this adulthood identity will stabilize their class trajectory. For former explorers and artists, this identity is poised to lift or maintain it.
33. Youth's incomes are likely to change even if their educations and the class of their occupations remains more stable. Income volatility is common while education and occupation volatility are less so (Western et al. 2012).

Appendix 1

1. This research uses data from the National Study of Youth and Religion (NSYR), a research project designed by Christian Smith, of the Department of Sociology at the University of Notre Dame, and generously funded by the Lilly Endowment Inc. of Indianapolis, Indiana.
2. For exceptions, see Armstrong and Hamilton (2013), Lareau (2011), and MacLeod (2008).
3. For example, studies by Willis (1977) and Bettie (2003) examine school-aged youth and infer how their respondents' class trajectories will unfold years into the future.
4. Of course, the NSYR has limitations for studying social mobility as well. Namely, it does not include data on parents' wealth. Its measure of parents' income is also limited in important ways. It includes only the income of residential parents and its highest parental income category is $100,000 and above. It also ends when respondents are young adults—not following them through middle age.
5. Though the survey included only 13-to-17-year-olds, by the time the interviews took place, some respondents had turned 18.
6. Kornrich and Furstenberg (2013); Reeves (2017).
7. The survey oversampled Jewish youth, and the interviews oversampled youth who attended private school and homeschool.
8. Lareau and Conley (2008).
9. I lightly edited the quotes from these interviews to enhance their readability—taking out "like" "um" and other filler words as well as false starts to sentences. I also lightly edited the original punctuation. I preserved the original meaning of each quote.
10. When the audio recordings failed, interviewers dictated the interview from memory and had their dictations transcribed.
11. This number comes from Michael Burrows's analysis of the PSID.
12. Killewald, Pfeffer, and Schachner (2017).
13. Schoeni and Ross (2005).
14. Wolff and Gittleman (2011).

15. Of course, it is possible that respondents simply did not bring up their parents' wealth. Still, it is unlikely that many respondents could count on receiving so much wealth from their parents that they would never have to work.
16. National Center for Education Statistics (2013), https://nces.ed.gov/programs/digest/d13/tables/dt13_211.60.asp.
17. Federal Reserve Bank of St. Louis (2017), https://fred.stlouisfed.org/series/MEPAINUSA672N.
18. Federal Reserve Bank of St. Louis (2017), https://fred.stlouisfed.org/series/MEHOINUSA672N?utm_source=series_page&utm_medium=related_content&utm_term=related_resources&utm_campaign=categories.
19. Sherman (2017).
20. Cooper (2014).
21. Timmermans and Tavory (2012).
22. These measures are admittedly crude. However, when youth make implicit conclusions about their likelihood to succeed in particular ways, they are more likely to develop a general sense of how they compare to their peers than one based on a careful analysis. Researchers with access to more detailed data could learn if more fine-grained distinctions matter.
23. Cahn and Carbone (2011).
24. Pew Research Center (2015).
25. One of the debates in cultural sociology is whether action is driven by goals or approaches. Those who take the approaches view tend to think of goals and approaches as only loosely connected. While respondents may not have been able to articulate the connection, youth with the same goals tended to take the same approaches.
26. Frank and Cook (1996).
27. Bourdieu (1980, 1984).

Appendix 3

1. Jenkins (1982); Streib (2017).
2. Jenkins (1982); Streib (2017).
3. Communities are akin to fields in that they established what is valued and the rules of the game.
4. Bourdieu (1980, 1984).
5. Toolkit theorists have suggested that focusing on identity would tell us why certain people use particular cultural tools more often than others (Swidler 2003, 2008). This book shows that which cultural tools people use does correspond to their identity. However, identities result from growing up in particular environments—ones with particular resources and expectations. And, to signal an identity, people must use the same tools consistently over time. If identities correspond to our social environment and lead us to use the same cultural tools over time, then what we have is more akin to a habitus than a toolkit.

6. Bourdieu (1988, 2000a) believed that downward mobility occurs through hysteresis: when sudden changes in the social world misalign the habitus with its new environment. Bourdieu considered hysteresis to be unusual. I show, instead, that generational and life course change make it so that aspects of the habitus are regularly misaligned with the environment.

7. This book follows what Vaisey (2010) called the seamless web's idea that if we dig deeper, we will find that culture coheres around particular environmental experiences. The "dig deeper" approach is out of vogue. In vogue is the idea that culture does not cohere so neatly around environmental experiences, so there is no need to look. However, it's worth pointing out that the "dig deeper" approach may not only be out of style for intellectual reasons. Sociologists are under pressure to publish more, and it is faster to identify what cultural tools individuals use than to discern if they cohere around a particular experience. In addition, the idea that we do not need to dig deeper comes out of the idea that people use culture in incoherent ways. However, people like the explorers may use cultural tools incoherently but do so in the same way over time—a fact that would correspond to the need to dig deeper. Of course, to see these patterns, we need longitudinal data, which also takes time to produce.

8. Bourdieu was not always explicit about defining class by fathers' occupation, but, when forced to operationalize class, this is often what he did. See, for example, Table A9 in *Distinction*. See also Silva (2005).

9. Sayer (2005:32). Sayer criticized the assumption of ontological complicity between the social environment and the habitus. My point is different. There is often ontological complicity between habitus and habitat—just habitat at a much more specific level than Bourdieu implied.

10. Bourdieu (1980, 1984). Lahire (2011) and Sayer (2005) also critiqued Bourdieu's idea that the habitus is neatly aligned with its childhood environment.

11. Bourdieu (1984) posited that the habitus is based upon individuals' class position relative to the entire class structure. However, Americans are notoriously misinformed about the degree of inequality between classes and about the lives of Americans not in their social class (Gimpelson and Treisman 2018). Their comparison group is then less likely to be their position in a country's class structure than it is to be their position compared to those around them. As social class segregation is common (Owens 2016; Reardon et al. 2018), youth will typically compare themselves to others in their social class.

12. Bourdieu acknowledged that different members of the same social class will have different resources and therefore different mobility trajectories. He wrote: "To say that the members of a class initially possessing a certain economic and cultural capital are destined, with a given probability, to an educational and social trajectory leading to a given position means in fact that a fraction of the class (which cannot be determined a priori with the limits of this explanatory system) will deviate from the trajectory most common for the class as a whole and follow the (higher or lower) trajectory which was most probable for members of another class" (Bourdieu 1984:111). However, not only did Bourdieu not focus on this point, but he did little to explain why some members of a fraction of a social class will have fewer resources than others.

13. Bourdieu most often referred to the family as children's primary socialization agent and the habitus as developing automatically from the direct and indirect socialization provided by a family and their class position. At times he hinted that family processes may vary. For example, he wrote: "the anticipations of the habitus, practical hypotheses based on past experience, give discorporate weight to early experiences. Through the economic and social necessity that they bring to bear on the relatively autonomous world of the domestic economy and family relations, or more precisely, through the specifically familial manifestations of this external necessity (forms of division of labor between the sexes, household objects, modes of consumption, parent-child relations, etc.), the structures characterizing a determinate class of conditions of existence produce the structures of the habitus, which in turn are the bases of the perception and appreciation of all subsequent experiences" (Bourdieu 1980:54). However, not only did Bourdieu not develop this idea, but he often also contradicted it. More often, he defined class origin by the father's occupation or set of capital, regulated women to being in charge of aesthetic labor, and failed to discuss relevant family processes (Silva 2005).

14. It is important not to reduce the transfer of parental resources to gender. In some families, mothers have more resources than fathers, and in some families, fathers are more hands-on than mothers.

15. Bourdieu and Passeron (1977); Bourdieu (1980, 1984).

16. Bourdieu (1988, 2000a).

17. In addition, some children may not be able to receive the resources parents try to transfer. This could occur in the case of children with learning disabilities, mental health issues, and physical health problems.

18. Opting out of what is denied was also Bourdieu's idea (Bourdieu and Passeron 1977; Bourdieu 1984).

19. Or, in Bourdieu's words, capital.

20. This difference can also help us explain variation in siblings' mobility trajectories. Not all siblings receive the same resources from their parents as their parents' resources and transference practices change over time.

21. Indeed, parents' occupation and education does not perfectly map onto their resources. It is possible that some working-class youth then grow up with more human, cultural, and economic capital than some upper-middle-class youth. Youth's identities can also quickly change how many resources they acquire. Working-class youth who identify as professionals may acquire more resources than some upper-middle-class youth who identify as stay-at-home mothers or rebels.

22. Michelle Obama's (Obama 2018) autobiography includes an example of this point. She was raised in a working-class family—by a stay-at-home mother and a city water plant employee. However, she recalled receiving many resources from her family and network. Her mother had a high degree of institutional knowledge and taught her how to navigate school to get ahead. Her grandfather had a high degree of academic knowledge and shared it with her. Her high school best friend, Jesse Jackson's daughter, inculcated her into the world of politics—teaching her how another institution worked. Though born into a working-class family, Michelle Obama grew up with

high levels of cultural and human capital. She developed a professional identity—describing herself as a "box checker" motivated by academic achievement. (At other times, she also described having an explorer identity—one that bounced between identifying as a professional and stay-at-home mother.)

23. If we define working-class as having a nonprofessional job and less than a four-year degree, then there is little room to fall. Income could differentiate the working class from the poor, but education and occupation would not.

24. Reay (2004).

25. Many researchers criticize the idea of the habitus for assuming that it is not conscious and reflexive (for example, see Archer 2007; Crossley 2001; Sayer 2005).

26. Some sociologists find toolkit theory to be more compelling than the idea of the habitus (Swidler 1986, 2003). What would this book look like through the lens of toolkit theory? We could see that youth who reproduced their class position used tools that correspond to the official purposes of school, college, and work. The official purposes of schools and colleges are to teach students and prepare them for the workforce. Those who reproduced their class position used corresponding tools such as focusing on academics, researching employers' expectations, and putting in long hours to build their knowledge and skills. Those who were downwardly mobile instead used cultural tools that corresponded to institutions' unofficial purposes—either exclusively or in combination with using cultural tools related to institutions' official purposes. The unofficial purposes of schools are to provide a place to meet romantic partners, socialize, pass time, and rebel. Youth who used strategies that corresponded to these purposes tended to be downwardly mobile. While this perspective may be helpful, it is limited. It veers close to being tautological and cannot explain why some people use different sets of tools than others. As such, it does not inform us about who is most likely to fall.

References

Abel, Jason, Richard Deitz, and Yaqin Su. 2014. "Are Recent College Graduates Finding Good Jobs?" *Current Issues in Economics and Finances* 20(1):1–8.

Alm, Susanne. 2011. "Downward Social Mobility across Generations: The Role of Parental Mobility and Education." *Sociological Research Online* 16(3):2.

Alon, Sigal. 2009. "The Evolution of Class Inequality in Higher Education: Competition, Exclusion, and Adaption." *American Sociological Review* 74(5):731–755.

Altintas, Evrim. 2016. "Widening Education-Gap in Development Childcare Activities in the U.S., 1965–2013." *Journal of Marriage and Family* 78(1):26–42.

Archer, Margaret. 2007. *Making Our Way Through the World: Human Reflexivity and Social Mobility*. Cambridge: Cambridge University Press.

Armstrong, Elizabeth and Laura Hamilton. 2013. *Paying for the Party: How College Maintains Inequality*. Cambridge, MA: Harvard University Press.

Arum, Richard and Josipa Roksa. 2010. *Academically Adrift: Limited Learning on College Campuses*. Chicago: University of Chicago Press.

Astin, Alexander and Leticia Oseguera. 2004. "The Declining 'Equity' of American Higher Education." *The Review of Higher Education* 27(3):321–341.

Autor, David. 2014. "Skills, Education, and the Rise of Earnings Inequality Among the 'Other 99 Percent.'" *Science* 344:843–851.

Avishai, Orit. 2008. "'Doing Religion' in a Secular World." *Gender & Society* 22(4):409–433.

Bailey, Martha and Susan Dynarski. 2011. "Inequality in Postsecondary Education." In Greg Duncan and Richard Murnane (eds.), *Whither Opportunity: Rising Inequality, Schools, and Children's Life Chances*, pp. 117–132. New York: Russell Sage.

Banta, Molly. 2015. "Why the Rich Stay Rich and the Poor Stay Poor." *Newsweek*, September 13.

Bartkowski, John and Christopher Ellison. 1995. "Divergent Models of Childrearing in Popular Manuals: Conservative Protestants vs. The Mainstream Experts." *Sociology of Religion* 56(1):21–34.

Bartkowski, John and Sarah Shah. 2014. "Religion and Gender Inequality: From Attitudes to Practices." In Lisa Keister and Darren Sherkat (eds.), *Religion and Inequality in America: Research and Theory on Religion's Role in Stratification*, pp. 173–194. New York: Cambridge University Press.

Bastedo, Michael and Ozan Jaquette. 2011. "Running in Place: Low-Income Students and the Dynamics of Higher Education Stratification." *Educational Evaluation and Policy Analysis* 33(3):318–339.

Beasley, Maya. 2011. *Opting Out: Losing the Potential of America's Young Black Elite*. Chicago: University Chicago Press.

Bell, Leslie. 2003. *Hard to Get: Twenty-Something Women and the Paradox of Sexual Freedom*. Berkeley: University of California Press.

Bellah, Robert, Richard Madsen, William Sullivan, Ann Swidler, and Steven Tipton. 2007. *Habits of the Heart: Individualism and Commitment in American Life.* Berkeley: University of California Press.

Beller, Emily and Michael Hout. 2006. "Intergenerational Social Mobility: The United States in Comparative Perspective." *The Future of Children* 16(2):19–36.

Bettie, Julie. 2003. *Women Without Class: Girls, Race, and Identity.* Berkeley: University of California Press.

Blair-Loy, Mary. 2003. *Competing Devotions: Career and Family Among Women Executives.* Cambridge, MA: Harvard University Press.

Bloome, Deirdre. 2015. "Income Inequality and Intergenerational Income Mobility in the United States." *Social Forces* 93(3):1047–1080.

Bloome, Deirdre. 2017. "Childhood Family Structure and Intergenerational Income Mobility in the United States." *Demography* 54(2):541–569.

Bloome, Deirdre, Christopher Muller, and Daniel Schrange. 2015. "Covariance Function Regressions for Studying Culture and Inequality." Population Association of America extended abstract.

Bourdieu, Pierre. 1980. *The Logic of Practice.* Cambridge, MA: Polity Press.

Bourdieu, Pierre. 1983. "The Field of Cultural Production, or The Economic World Reversed." *Poetics* 12(4–5):311–356.

Bourdieu, Pierre. 1984. *Distinction: A Social Critique of the Judgment of Taste.* Cambridge, MA: Harvard University Press.

Bourdieu, Pierre. 1986. "The Forms of Capital." In J. E. Richardson (ed.), *Handbook of Theory of Research for the Sociology of Education,* pp. 241–258. Westport, CT: Greenwood Press.

Bourdieu, Pierre. 1988. *Homo Academicus.* Cambridge: Polity Press.

Bourdieu, Pierre. 2000a. *Pascalian Meditations.* Cambridge: Polity Press.

Bourdieu, Pierre. 2000b. *The Weight of the World: Social Suffering in Contemporary Society.* Palo Alto: Stanford University Press.

Bourdieu, Pierre and Jean-Claude Passeron. 1977. *Reproduction in Education, Society, and Culture.* New York: Sage.

Bowen, William, Martin Kurzweil, and Eugene Tobin. 2005. *Equity and Excellence in American Higher Education.* Charlottesville: University of Virginia Press.

Bowles, Samuel and Herbert Gintis. 1976. *Schooling in Capitalist America: Educational Reform and the Contradictions of Economic Life.* New York: Basic Books.

Buchmann, Claudia, Dennis Condron, and Vincent Roscigno. 2010. "Shadow Education, American Style: Test Preparation, the SAT and College Enrollment." *Social Forces* 89(2):435–462.

Buss, David, Todd Shackelford, Lee Kirkpatrick, and Randy Larsen. 2001. "A Half Century of Mate Preferences: The Cultural Evolution of Values." *Journal of Marriage and Family* 63(2):491–503.

Cahn, Naomi and June Carbone. 2011. *Red Families vs. Blue Families: Legal Polarization and the Creation of Culture.* New York: Oxford University Press.

Calarco, Jessica. 2018. *Negotiated Opportunities: How the Middle Class Secures Advantages in School.* New York: Oxford University Press.

Carlson, Allan. 1996. "Gender, Children, and Social Labor: Transcending the 'Family Wage' Dilemma." *Journal of Social Issues* 52(3):137–161.

Cha, Youngjoo. 2010. "Reinforcing Separate Spheres: The Effect of Spousal Overwork on the Employment of Men and Women in Dual-Earner Households." *American Sociological Review* 75(2):303–329.

Chambliss, Daniel. 1989. "The Mundanity of Excellence: An Ethnographic Report on Stratification and Olympic Swimmers." *Sociological Theory* 7(1):70–86.

Charlton, Linda. 1973. "Home Loan Panel Upholds Women's Mortgage Right." *New York Times*, December 18.

Cherlin, Andrew. 2010. *The Marriage-Go-Round: The State of Marriage and the Family in America*. New York: Vintage.

Chetty, Raj, David Grusky, Maximilian Hell, Nathaniel Hendren, Robert Manduca, and Jimmy Narang. 2018. "The Fading American Dream: Trends in Absolute Income Mobility Since 1940s." NBER Working Paper 22910.

Clark, Burton and Martin Trow. 1966. "The Organizational Context." In Theodore Newcomb and Everett Wilson (eds.), *College Peer Groups: Problems and Prospects for Research*, pp. 17–70. Chicago: Aldine.

Coe, Alexis. 2013. "Dads Caring for Their Kids: It's Parenting, Not Babysitting." *The Atlantic*, January 23.

Coltrane, Scott. 1997. *Family Man: Fatherhood, Housework, and Gender Equity*. New York: Oxford University Press.

Coltrane, Scott and Michele Adams. 1997. "Children and Gender." In Terry Arendell (ed.), *Contemporary Parenting*, pp. 219–253. Thousand Oaks, CA: Sage.

Conley, Dalton. 2005. *The Pecking Order: Which Siblings Succeed and Why*. New York: Pantheon Books.

Coontz, Stephanie. 1997. *The Way We Really Are: Coming to Terms with America's Changing Families*. New York: Basic Books.

Coontz, Stephanie. 2013. "Why Gender Inequality Stalled." *New York Times*, February 16.

Coontz, Stephanie. 2016. *The Way We Never Were: American Families and the Nostalgia Trap*. New York: Basic Books.

Cooper, Marianne. 2014. *Cut Adrift: Families in Insecure Times*. Berkeley: University of California Press.

Crittenden, Ann. 2010. *The Price of Motherhood: Why the Most Important Job in the World Is Still the Least Valued*. New York: Picador.

Crossley, Nick. 2001. "The Phenomenological Habitus and Its Construction." *Theory and Society* 30(1):81–120.

Currid-Halkett, Elizabeth. 2017. *The Sum of Small Things: A Theory of the Aspirational Class*. Princeton: Princeton University Press.

Den Hartog, Arie. 1985. "The Christian Family: The Role of Husband and Father." *Standard Bearer* 61(20): September 1.

Dobson, James. 2007. *Straight Talk to Men: Timeless Principles for Leading Your Family*. Carol Stream, IL: Tyndale House.

Dobson, James. N.d. "Dr. James Dobson's 90 Second Commentary, May 11: A Father's Role." https://www.drjamesdobson.org/Broadcasts/my-family-talk-dr-james-dobson-Broadcast?i=c5c68108-3f73-4c10-b407-3a247944fdc9.

Edgell, Penny. 2006. *Religion and Family in a Changing Society*. Princeton: Princeton University Press.

Ehrenreich, Barbara. 1989. *Fear of Falling: The Inner Life of the Middle Class*. New York: Harper Perennial.

Eikhof, Doris and Chris Warhurst. 2013. "The Promised Land? Why Social Inequalities Are Systemic in the Creative Industries." *Employee Relations* 35(5):495–508.

England, Paula. 2010. "The Gender Revolution: Stalled and Unequal." *Gender & Society* 24(2):149–166.

Evans, Lorraine and Kimberly Davies. 2000. "No Sissy Boys Here: A Content Analysis of the Representation of Masculinity in Elementary School Reading Textbooks." *Sex Roles* 42(3/4):255–270.

Federal Reserve Bank of St. Louis. 2017. "Real Median Personal Income in the United States." https://fred.stlouisfed.org/series/MEPAINUSA672N.

Ferrare, Joseph. 2016. "Intergenerational Education Mobility Trends by Race and Gender in the United States." *AERA Open* 2(4):1–17.

Flanagan, Caitlin. 2014. "The Dark Power of Fraternities." *The Atlantic.* March.

Flouri, Eirini and Ann Buchanan. 2004. "Early Father's and Mother's Involvement and Child's Later Educational Outcomes." *British Journal of Educational Psychology* 74(2):141–153.

Fontenault, Tim. 2010. "For the Love of the Game: Five Athletes We Can All Learn From." *The Bleacher Report*, August 21. https://bleacherreport.com/articles/440416-for-love-of-the-game-five-athletes-we-can-all-learn-from#slide2.

Fortin, Nicole. 2005. "Gender Role Attitudes and the Labour-Market Outcomes of Women Across OCED Countries." *Oxford Review of Economic Policy* 21(3):416–438.

Frank, Robert and Philip Cook. 1996. *The Winner-Take-All Society: Why the Few at the Top Get So Much More Than the Rest of Us.* New York: Penguin Random House.

Furstenberg, Frank. 2008. "The Intersections of Social Class and the Transition to Adulthood." *New Directions for Child and Adolescent Development* 119:1–10.

Gallagher, Sally. 2004. "The Marginalization of Evangelical Feminism." *Sociology of Religion* 65(3):215–237.

Gallagher, Sally and Christian Smith. 1999. "Symbolic Traditionalism and Pragmatic Egalitarianism: Contemporary Evangelicals, Families, and Gender." *Gender & Society* 13(2):211–233.

Gerstel, Naomi and Natalia Sarkisian. 2006. "Marriage: The Good, the Bad, and the Greedy." *Contexts* 5(4):16–22.

Giddens, Anthony. 1991. *Modernity and Self-Identity: Self and Society in the Late Modern Age.* Palo Alto: Stanford University Press.

Gimpelson, Vladimir and Daniel Treisman. 2018. "Misperceiving Inequality." *Economics & Politics* 30(1):27–54.

Goldin, Claudia. 1988. "Marriage Bars: Discrimination Against Women Workers, 1920s to 1950s." NBER Working Paper No. 2724.

Grodsky, Eric and Catherine Riegle-Crumb. 2010. "Those Who Choose and Those Who Don't: Social Background and College Orientation." *Annals of the American Academy of Political and Social Science* 627(1):14–35.

Grusky, David, Bruce Western, and Christopher Wimer. 2011. *The Great Recession.* New York: Russell Sage Foundation.

Guilder, George. 1986. "Women in the Work Force." *The Atlantic*, September.

Hamilton, Laura. 2016. *Parenting to a Degree: How Family Matters for College Women's Success.* Chicago: University of Chicago Press.

Hart, Betty and Todd Risley. 1995. *Meaningful Differences in the Everyday Experiences of Young American Children.* Baltimore: Paul H. Brookes.

Hays, Sharon. 1996. *The Cultural Contradictions of Motherhood.* New Haven: Yale University Press.

Heiman, Rachel. 2015. *Driving After Class: Anxious Times in an American Suburb.* Berkeley: University of California Press.

Heller, Donald and Patricia Marin. 2002. *Who Should We Help? The Negative Consequences of Merit Scholarships.* Cambridge: Harvard Civil Rights Foundation.

Hertel, Florian. 2017. *Social Mobility in the 20th Century: Class Mobility and Occupational Change in the United States and Germany.* Florence, Italy: Springer.

Hertel, Florian and Olaf Groh-Samberg. 2014. "Class Mobility Across Three Generations in the U.S. and Germany." *Research in Social Stratification and Mobility* 35:35–52.

Hochschild, Jennifer. 1995. *Facing Up to the American Dream: Race, Class, and the Soul of the Nation.* Princeton: Princeton University Press.

Horowitz, Jonathan. 2018. "Relative Education and the Advantage of a College Degree." *American Sociological Review* 83(4):771–801.

Houle, Jason. 2014. "A Generation Indebted Young Adult Debt Across Three Cohorts." *Social Problems* 61(3):448–465.

Hout, Michael. 2019. "Social Mobility." *Pathways: The Poverty and Inequality Report,* 29–32.

Hout, Michael and Alexander Janus. 2011. "Educational Mobility in the United States Since the 1930s." In Greg Duncan and Richard Murnane (eds.), *Whither Opportunity: Rising Inequality, Schools, and Children's Life Chances,* pp. 165–186. New York: Russell Sage.

Hoxby, Caroline. 2009. "The Changing Selectivity of American Colleges." *Journal of Economic Perspectives* 23(4):95–118.

Illouz, Eva. 2008. *Saving the Modern Soul: Therapy, Emotions, and the Culture of Self-Help.* Berkeley: University of California Press.

Ispa-Landa, Simone. 2013. "Gender, Race, and Justifications for Group Exclusion: Urban Black Students Bussed to Affluent Suburban Schools." *Sociology of Education* 86(3):218–233.

Jacobs, Jerry and Kathleen Gerson. 2004. *The Time Divide.* Cambridge, MA: Harvard University Press.

Jacobs, Jerry and Kathleen Gerson. 2015. "Unpacking Americans' Views of the Employment of Mothers and Fathers Using National Vignette Survey Data." *Gender & Society* 30(3):413–441.

Jenkins, Richard. 1982. "Pierre Bourdieu and the Reproduction of Determinism." *Sociology* 16(2):270–281.

Jerolmack, Colin and Shamus Khan. 2014. "Talk Is Cheap: Ethnography and the Attitudinal Fallacy." *Sociological Methods & Research* 43(2):178–209.

Kahlenberg, Richard. 2010. *Affirmative Action for the Rich: Legacy Preferences in College Admissions.* New York: Century Foundation Press.

Kalmijn, Matthijs. 1994. "Mother's Occupational Status and Children's Schooling." *American Sociological Review* 59(2):257–275.

Karabel, Jerome. 2005. *The Chosen: The Hidden History of Admission and Exclusion at Harvard, Yale, and Princeton.* Boston: Houghton Mifflin.

Kearney, Melissa and Phillip Levine. 2015. "Economic Despair: The Vicious Circle of Inequality and Social Mobility." *Brookings,* May 29.

Keister, Lisa and Darren E. Sherkat. 2014. *Religion and Inequality.* New York: Cambridge University Press.

Killewald, Alexandra, Fabian Pfeffer, and Jared Schachner. 2017. "Wealth Inequality and Accumulation." *Annual Review of Sociology* 43:379–404.

Kimmel, Michael. 2008. *Guyland: The Perilous World Where Boys Become Men.* New York: Harper Collins.

Kornrich, Sabino and Frank Furstenberg. 2013. "Investing in Children: Changes in Parental Spending on Children, 1972–2007." *Demography* 50(1):1–23.

Kusserow, Adrie. 2004. *American Individualisms: Child Rearing and Social Class in Three Neighborhoods.* New York: Palgrave MacMillan.

Lacy, Karyn. 2007. *Blue-Chip Black: Race, Class, and Status in the New Black Middle Class.* Berkeley: University of California Press.

Lahire, Bernard. 2011. *The Plural Actor.* New York: Wiley.

Lamont, Ellen. 2020. *The Mating Game: How Gender Still Shapes How We Date.* Oakland: University of California Press.

Lareau, Annette. 1989. *Home Advantage: Social Class and Parental Intervention in Elementary Education.* Lanham, MD: Rowan and Littlefield.

Lareau, Annette. 2011. *Unequal Childhoods: Class, Race, and Family Life.* 2nd ed. Berkeley: University of California Press.

Lareau, Annette and Dalton Conley. 2008. *Social Class: How Does It Work?* New York: Russell Sage.

Lareau, Annette, Elliot Weininger, and Amanda Cox. 2018. "Parental Challenges to Organizational Authority in an Elite School District: The Role of Cultural, Social, and Symbolic Capital." *Teachers College Record* 120(1):1–46.

Laurin, Kristin and Holly Engstrom. 2020. "The Context of Low Socioeconomic Status Can Undermine People's Motivation for Financial Success." *Current Opinion in Psychology* 33:105–109.

Levey-Friedman, Hilary. 2013. *Playing to Win: Raising Children in a Competitive Culture.* Berkeley: University of California Press.

Lingo, Elizabeth and Stephen Tepper. 2013. "Looking Back, Looking Forward: Arts-Based Careers and Creative Work." *Work and Occupations* 40(4):337–363.

Lundberg, Shelly. 2005. "Sons, Daughters, and Parental Behavior." *Oxford Review of Economic Policy* 21(3):340–356.

MacLeod, Jay. 2008. *Ain't No Makin' It: Aspirations an Attainment in a Low-Income Neighborhood.* 3rd ed. Boulder: Westview Press.

Mare, Robert. 2015. "Educational Homogamy in Two Gilded Ages: Evidence from Inter-Generational Social Mobility Data." *Annals of the American Academy of Political and Social Science* 663(1):117–139.

Mahoney, Annette, Kenneth Pargament, Aaron Murray-Swank, and Nichole Murray-Swank. 2003. "Religion and the Sanctification of Family Relationships." *Review of Religious Research* 44(3):220–236.

Marini, Matteo and Patrick Mooney. 2006. "Rural Economies." In Paul Cloake, Terry Marsden, and Patrick Mooney (eds.), *The Handbook of Rural Studies*, pp. 91–103. Thousand Oakes, CA: Sage.

Mathur, Aparna and Cody Kallen. 2017. "Poor Rich Kids? The Mysterious Decline in Mobility at the Top." *Forbes*, May 4.

McCall, Leslie. 2013. *The Undeserving Rich: American Beliefs About Inequality, Opportunity, and Redistribution.* Cambridge: Cambridge University Press.

McGinn, Kathleen, Mayra Ruiz Castro, Elizabeth Long Lingo. 2019. "Learning from Mum: Cross-National Evidence Linking Maternal Employment and Adult Children's Outcomes." *Work, Employment and Society* 33(3):374–400.

McLanahan, Sara and Gary Sandefur. 1994. *Growing Up With a Single Parent.* Cambridge, MA: Harvard University Press.

Menger, Pierre-Michel. 1999. "Artistic Labor Markets and Careers." *Annual Review of Sociology* 25:541–574.

Messineo, Joe. 2016. "For Love of the Game, or the Money." *The Sports Post*, July 7. https://thesportspost.com/nfl-nba-athletes-big-money-motives/.

Metzgar, Jack. 2019. "Achieving Mediocrity." Unpublished Manuscript.

Miles, Matthew, A. Michael Huberman, and Johnny Saldaña. 2014. *Qualitative Data Analysis: A Methods Sourcebook.* Thousand Oaks, CA: Sage.

Mitnik, Pablo, Erin Cumberworth, and David Grusky. 2015. "Social Mobility in a High-Income Regime." *Annals of the American Academy of Political and Social Science* 663(1):140–184.

Mullen, Ann. 2010. *Degrees of Inequality: Culture, Class and Gender in American Higher Education.* Baltimore: John Hopkins University Press.

Murnane, Richard and Sean Reardon. 2018. "Long-Term Trends in Private School Enrollments by Family Income." *AERA Open* 4(1):1–24.

National Center for Educational Statistics. 2013. "Estimated Average Annual Salary of Teachers in Public Elementary and Secondary Schools, by State: 1969–70 Through 2012–13." *Digest of Educational Statistics*, https://nces.ed.gov/programs/digest/d13/tables/dt13_211.60.asp.

Newman, Katherine. 1988. *Falling from Grace: The Experience of Downward Mobility in the American Middle Class.* Berkeley: University of California Press.

Obama, Michelle. 2018. *Becoming.* New York: Crown.

Oppenheimer, Valerie. 1988. "A Theory of Marriage Timing." *American Journal of Sociology* 94(3):563–591.

Owens, Ann. 2016. "Inequality in Children's Contexts Income Segregation of Households With and Without Children." *American Sociological Review* 81(3):549–574.

Parcel, Toby and Elizabeth Menaghan. 1994. "Early Parental Work, Family Social Capital, and Early Childhood Outcomes." *American Journal of Sociology* 99(4):972–1009.

Parker, Kim and Gretchen Livingston. 2017. "6 Facts About American Fathers." *Pew Research Center Fact Tank*, June 15. http://www.pewresearch.org/fact-tank/2017/06/15/fathers-day-facts/.

Pearce, Lisa and Arland Thornton. 2007. "Religious Identity and Family Ideologies in the Transition to Adulthood." *Journal of Marriage and Family* 69(5):1227–1243.

Pérez-Peña, Richard. 2014. "What You Don't Know About Financial Aid (but Should)." *New York Times*, April 9.

Pew Research Center. 2015. "America's Changing Religious Landscape. Appendix B: Classification of Protestant Denominations." http://www.pewforum.org/2015/05/12/appendix-b-classification-of-protestant-denominations/.

Pew Research Center. 2017. "How Income Volatility Interacts With American Families' Financial Security." March 9. https://www.pewtrusts.org/en/research-and-analysis/issue-briefs/2017/03/how-income-volatility-interacts-with-american-families-financial-security.

Posselt, Julie and Eric Grodsky. 2017. "Graduate Education and Social Stratification." *Annual Review of Sociology* 43:353–378.

Putnam, Robert. 2015. *Our Kids: The American Dream in Crisis.* New York: Simon and Schuster.

Raley, R. Kelly, Megan Sweeney, and Danielle Wondra. 2015. "The Growing Racial and Ethnic Divide in US Marriage Patterns." *The Future of Children* 25(2):89–109.

Rampell, Catherine. 2011. "The Haves and the Have-Notes." *New York Times*, January 31.

Reardon, Sean, Kendra Bischoff, Ann Owens, and Joseph Townsend. 2018. "Has Income Segregation Really Increased? Bias and Bias Correction in Sample-Based Segregation Estimates." *Demography* 55(6):2129–2160.

Reay, Diane. 2004. "'It's All Becoming Habitus': Beyond the Habitual Use of Habitus in Educational Research." *British Journal of Sociology of Education* 25(4):431–444.

Reeves, Richard. 2017. *Dream Hoarders: How the American Upper Middle Class Is Leaving Everyone Else in the Dust, Why That Is a Problem, And What to Do About It.* Washington, DC: Brookings Institute.

Rice, Tom and Diane Coates. 1995. "Gender Role Attitudes in the Southern United States." *Gender & Society* 9(6):744–756.

Rios, Victor. 2009. "The Consequences of the Criminal Justice Pipeline on Black and Latino Masculinity." *Annals of the American Academy of Political and Social Sciences* 623(1):150–162.

Rivera, Lauren. 2015. *Pedigree: How Elite Students Get Elite Jobs.* Princeton: Princeton University Press.

Roscigno, Vincent, Donald Tomaskovic-Devey, and Martha Crowley. 2006. "Education and the Inequalities of Place." *Social Forces* 84(4):2121–2145.

Rose, Deondra. 2015. "Regulating Opportunity: Title IX and the Birth of Gender-Conscious Higher Education Policy." *Journal of Policy History* 27(1):157–183.

Santoli, Susan. 2002. "Is There an Advanced Placement Advantage?" *American Secondary Education* 30(3):23–35.

Sayer, Andrew. 2005. *The Moral Significance of Class.* Cambridge: Cambridge University Press.

Sayer, Liana, Suzanne Bianchi, and John Robinson. 2004. "Are Parents Investing Less in Children? Trends in Mothers' and Fathers' Time with Children." *American Journal of Sociology* 110(1):1–43.

Schoeni, Robert and Karen Ross. 2005. "Material Assistance Received from Families During the Transition to Adulthood." In Richard Settersten, Jr., Frank Furstenberg, Jr., and Ruben Rumbaut (eds.), *On the Frontier of Adulthood: Theory, Research, and Public Policy*, pp. 396–416. Chicago: University of Chicago Press.

Schoeni, Robert and Emily Wiemers. 2015. "The Implications of Selective Attrition for Estimates of Intergenerational Elasticity of Family Income." *Journal of Economic Inequality* 13(3):351–372.

Schrock, Douglas and Michael Schwalbe. 2009. "Men, Masculinity, and Manhood Acts." *Annual Review of Sociology* 35:277–295.

Schwartz, Christine and Robert Mare. 2005. "Trends in Educational Assortative Marriage from 1940 to 2003." *Demography* 42(4):621–646.

Settersten, Richard and Barbara Ray. 2010. "What's Going on With Young People Today? The Long and Twisting Path to Adulthood." *The Future of Children* 20(1):19–41.

Shapiro, Robert. 2018. "The New Economics of Jobs Is Bad News for Working-Class Americans—and Maybe for Trump." Brookings Institute, https://www.brookings.edu/blog/fixgov/2018/01/16/the-new-economics-of-jobs-is-bad-news-for-working-class-americans-and-maybe-for-trump/.

Sherkat, Darren. 2000. "'That They Be Keepers of the Home': The Effect of Conservative Religion on Early and Late Transitions into Housewifery." *Review of Religious Research* 41(3):344–358.

Sherman, Rachel. 2017. *Uneasy Street: The Anxieties of Affluence*. Princeton: Princeton University Press.

Silva, Elizabeth. 2005. "Gender, Home and Family in Cultural Capital Theory." *The British Journal of Sociology* 56(1):83–103.

Small, Mario, David Harding, and Michèle Lamont. 2010. "Reconsidering Culture and Poverty." *Annals of the American Academy of Political and Social Sciences* 629(1):6–27.

Sperber, Murray. 2001. *Beer and Circus: How Big-Time College Sports Is Crippling Undergraduate Education*. New York: Holt.

Stephens-Davidowitz, Seth. 2017. *Everybody Lies: Big Data, New Data, and What the Internet Can Tell Us About Who We Really Are*. New York: Dey Street Books.

Stevens, Mitchell. 2009. *Creating a Class: College Admissions and the Education of Elites*. Cambridge, MA: Harvard University Press.

Stone, Pamela. 2007. *Opting Out? Why Women Really Quit Careers and Head Home*. Berkeley: University of California Press.

Streib, Jessi. 2015. *The Power of the Past: Understanding Cross-Class Marriages*. New York: Oxford University Press.

Streib, Jessi. 2017. "The Unbalanced Theoretical Toolkit: Problems and Partial Solutions to Studying Culture and Reproduction but not Culture and Mobility." *American Journal of Cultural Sociology* 5(1–2):127–153.

Stuber, Jenny. 2011. *Inside the College Gates: Class, Culture, and Higher Education*. Lanham, MD: Lexington Books.

Swidler, Ann. 1986. "Culture in Action: Symbols and Strategies." *American Sociological Review* 51(2):273–286.

Swidler, Ann. 2003. *Talk of Love: How Culture Matters*. Chicago: University of Chicago Press.

Swidler, Ann. 2008. "Comment on Stephen Vaisey's 'Socrates, Skinner, and Aristotle: Three Ways of Thinking About Culture in Action.'" *Sociological Forum* 23(3):614–618.

Taylor, Lorraine, Jennifer Clayton, and Stephanie Rowley. 2004. "Academic Socialization: Understanding Parental Influences on Children's School-Related Development in the Early Years." *Review of General Psychology* 8(3):163–178.

The Economist. 2015. "An Hereditary Meritocracy: America's Elite." January 24.

The Church of Jesus Christ of Latter-Day Saints. N.d. *Eternal Marriage Student Manual*. Salt Lake City, Utah. https://www.lds.org/bc/content/shared/content/english/pdf/language-materials/35311_eng.pdf?lang=eng.

Thijssen, Lex and Maarten Wolbers. 2016. "Determinants of Intergenerational Downward Mobility in the Netherlands." *Social Indicators Research* 128(3):995–1010.

Thomas, Melvin. 1993. "Race, Class, and Personal Income: An Empirical Test of the Declining Significance of Race Thesis, 1968–1988." *Social Problem* 40(3):328–342.

Thompson, Derek. 2014. "Economists: Your Parents Are More Important Than Ever." *The Atlantic*, January 23.

Timmermans, Stephan and Tavory, Iddo. 2012. "Theory Construction in Qualitative Research: From Grounded Theory to Abductive Analysis." *Sociological Theory* 30(3):167–186.

Torche, Florencia. 2011. "Is a College Degree Still the Great Equalizer? Intergenerational Mobility Across Levels of Schooling in the United States." *American Journal of Sociology* 117(3):763–807.

Turner, Jonathan. 2014. "Emotions and Societal Stratification." In Jan Stets and Jonathan Turner (eds.), *Handbook of Sociology of Emotions*. Vol. 2: *Handbooks of Sociology and Social Research*. Dordrecht: Springer.

Uecker, Jeremy and Lisa Pearce. 2017. "Conservative Protestantism and Horizontal Stratification in Education: The Case of College Selectivity." *Social Forces* 96(2):661–689.

Uecker, Jeremy and Charles Stokes. 2008. "Early Marriage in the United States." *Journal of Marriage and Family* 70(4):835–846.

US Census Bureau. 2001. "Current Population Reports, P60-213, Money Income in the United States: 2000." Washington, DC: US Government Printing Office.

Vaisey, Stephen. 2006. "Education and Its Discontents: Overqualification in America, 1972–2002." *Social Forces* 85(2):835–864.

Vaisey, Stephen. 2009. "Motivation and Justification: A Dual-Process Model of Culture in Action." *American Journal of Sociology* 114(6):1675–1715.

Vaisey, Stephen. 2010. "What People Want: Rethinking Poverty, Culture, and Educational Attainment." *Annals of the American Academy of Political and Social Science* 629(1):75–101.

Waite, Linda and Mark Nielsen. 2001. "The Rise of the Dual-Earner Family, 1963–1997." In Rosanna Hertz and Nancy Marshall (eds), *Working Families: The Transformation of the American Home*, pp. 23–41. Berkeley: University of California Press.

Walkerdine, Valerie, Helen Lucey, and June Melody. 2001. *Growing Up Girl: Psychosocial Explorations of Gender and Class*. New York: New York University Press.

Western, Bruce, Deirdre Bloome, Benjamin Sosnaud, and Laura Tach. 2012. "Economic Insecurity and Social Stratification." *American Review of Sociology* 8:341–359.

Wilderman, Christopher and Bruce Western. 2010. "Incarceration in Fragile Families." *The Future of Children* 20(2):157–177.

Williams, David. 1999. "Race, Socioeconomic Status, and Health: The Added Effects of Racism and Discrimination." *Annals of the New York Academy of Sciences* 896:173–188.

Willis, Paul. 1977. *Learning to Labor: How Working-Class Kids Get Working-Class Jobs*. Aldershot, UK: Gower.

Wilson, William Julius. 2009. *More Than Just Race: Being Black and Poor in the Inner City*. New York: W. W. Norton.

Wing-Fai, Leung Rosalind Gill, and Keith Randle. 2015. "Getting In, Getting On, Getting Out? Women as Career Scramblers in the UK Film and Television Industries." *The Sociological Review* 63(1):50–65.

Wodtke, Geoffrey. 2015. "Continuity and Change in the American Class Structure: Workplace Ownership and Authority Relations from 1972 to 2010." *Research in Stratification and Mobility* 42:48–61.

Woods, Mark. 2015. "Is Pope Francis Right? Is it Wrong for Christians to be Ambitious?" *Christian Today*, October 19.

Wolff, Edward and Maury Gittleman. 2011. "Inheritances and the Distribution of Wealth or Whatever Happened to the Great Inheritance Boom?" BLS Working Papers. US Bureau of Labor Statistics.

Zarifa, David, Jeannie Kim, Brad Seward, and David Walters. 2018. "What's Taking You So Long? Examining the Effects of Social Class on Completing a Bachelor's Degree in Four Years." *Sociology of Education* 91(4):290–322.

Index